How to be a Poet

How to be a Poet

Jo Bell and Jane Commane

with special guest writers

Nine
Arches
Press

How to be a Poet
Jo Bell and Jane Commane

ISBN: 978-1-911027-11-9

First published December 2017 by:

Nine Arches Press
PO Box 6269
Rugby
CV21 9NL
United Kingdom

www.ninearchespress.com

Printed in Britain by:
Imprint Digital

Nine Arches Press is supported using public funding by the National Lottery through Arts Council England.

Supported using public funding by
**ARTS COUNCIL
ENGLAND**

About the Authors:

Jo Bell is a poet, tutor and begetter of poetry projects. Her 52 project became an online phenomenon and the writing prompts from the project were published in the handbook *52: Write a Poem a Week. Start Now. Keep Going* (Nine Arches Press). Her poetry collections are *Navigation* (now available as an eBook) and *Kith* (Nine Arches Press). Jo was born in Sheffield and grew up on the fringes of the Derbyshire Peak District, leaving school just after the Miners' Strike. She became an industrial archaeologist, specialising in coal and lead mines. A winner of the Charles Causley Prize and the Manchester Cathedral Prize, Jo was the inaugural Canal Laureate for the UK, appointed by the Poetry Society and the Canal & River Trust. She lives on a narrowboat on the English waterways.

Jane Commane was born in Coventry and lives and works in Warwickshire. Her first poetry collection is *Assembly Lines* (Bloodaxe, 2018). Her poetry has featured in anthologies including *The Best British Poetry 2011* (Salt Publishing) and *Lung Jazz: Young British Poets for Oxfam* (Cinnamon) and in magazines including *Anon, And Other Poems, Bare Fiction, Iota, Tears in the Fence* and *The North*. In 2016, she was chosen to join Writing West Midlands' Room 204 writer development programme. Jane is editor at Nine Arches Press, co-editor of *Under the Radar* magazine, and co-organiser of the Leicester Shindig poetry series. In 2017, she was awarded a Jerwood Compton Poetry Fellowship.

CONTENTS

A note to our readers:

The chapters titled 'On...' are by Jo Bell, and those titled 'How to...' are by Jane Commane.

Other chapters by our guest writers are named accordingly.

We have tried to ensure, where possible, that we offer our readers low-cost and free ways to explore poetry, and advise where funding or bursaries can be of use. Please see the back pages of this book for a list of useful links to organisations who can help. We don't believe that learning to write well should be expensive or exclusive. The pleasure of enjoying good poetry should be open to all.

Welcome to *How to be a Poet*

Reader, we have got you between the covers on a false pretext. This is not exactly a 'how to' manual. It will not tell you how many lines there are in a sonnet (fourteen) or give you the structure of a sestina (too long to explain here). For guidance like that there are many books available. What we wanted to do here is to give you a kind of handbook for the poetry life; not how to write poems, but how to be a poet in twenty-first century culture.

How to be a Poet is a manifesto of sorts. It is an exploration, both practically and creatively, of what it is to write poems, read poems, share poems and publish poetry. It is a guide to writing well, and aims to be bold and up-front about the realities of writing poetry and being a poet in the here and now. It contains advice, but also a healthy dose of myth-busting, plenty of challenging ideas and some thought-provoking proposals that are designed to stretch both new and more experienced writers of poetry. It won't pull any punches. It is a Poem-Writer's Guide to the Galaxy.

What isn't *How to be a Poet* about?
It isn't a step by step fail-safe plan for poetry success. It won't write the poems for you. It doesn't aim to make you an award-winning poet by the power of its advice alone, and that's really not what poetry writing should be about, anyway. It won't guarantee that it can get your first book of poems published, though that may come to pass as a happy offshoot of helping to make you a better poet overall. And there will be plenty of thoughts on what exactly that means, and how we can strive to write, read and participate better as poets.

Much of this book is also about **granting yourself permission**, and equipping you with the ideas and knowledge that will help to make your participation in poetry as an art form more fulfilling, life-enriching and creatively satisfying.

There are certainly some guidelines on writing here, and a good deal of advice on editing; but we also include advice on how to tackle difficult subjects or revisit a poem that isn't working. There is practical guidance to help you make good use of social media, submit work to journals and get your poetry into print. Above all, the two skills we celebrate and encourage most are those of looking at the world in a receptive state of mind, and of reading poetry as often as you write it.

We have divided these topics according to our own interests and experience. Jo Bell is a poet and begetter of poetry projects, such as the online community 52 which shepherded hundreds of poets into better writing practices. She has taught hundreds of poetry courses for organisations including The Poetry School and the Arvon Foundation, and is widely published in print and online. Her sections in this book are headed 'On....' and are concerned with writerly practice. Jane Commane, also a poet, appears here more in the light of being a successful poetry publisher (she heads Nine Arches Press) and the co-editor of well-regarded poetry journal *Under the Radar*. She is a promoter of poetry events, a successful seeker of funding, and known as an incisive editor of poetry on the page. Her chapters are headed 'How to....' and deal mainly with the practical issues of getting your poems in front of a wider readership.

In the process of writing this book we've learned a lot about our own opinions, and have crystallised much of our own thinking about what works best in creative and practical terms. We hope you find it useful, and we hope it will sit on your bookshelf in good company with the poets of this age and previous ages, who will always be your best teachers. We hope most of all that you find this book to be a thought-provoking companion.

Jo Bell and Jane Commane, November 2017.

CHAPTER ONE
On Your Marks...

Let's get this out of the way. Can we teach someone How to be a Poet? The answer is crystal clear.

No.

And yes. This project isn't called *How to Write a Poem*, or *How to Get Your Poetry Published*, though we'll talk at some length about both. It isn't called *Get Rich Writing Poetry* because nobody knows how to do that. We called our project *How to Be a Poet* because it's not just a writing manual. It's an offering up of our own thoughts on the practice of poetry; a consideration of what poetry reading and writing can mean to a thoughtful person seeking to do both with pleasure and skill.

Certainly we can and will teach you useful things about technique. Certainly we can give shortcuts that will save you a lot of time in hitting your stride on the page, and help you to avoid the common pitfalls of writing – the traps of cliché, of being derivative, of sloppy editing. We're well qualified. Between us we have helped hundreds of people to write like their best selves, and there is a stream of award-winning work from the poets we've worked with to prove it. We have also made (and continue to make) the mistakes we're going to try and talk you out of. In poetry as in life, no-one stops learning.

Our book is only one of many you could read. Stephen King's *On Writing*, Glyn Maxwell's *On Poetry*, Joyce Carol Oates' *The Faith of a Writer*, Ted Hughes' *Poetry in the Making*, Robin Behn's *The Practice of Poetry* – there's no need to rush at the reading list. You will never get to the end of it, because some blighter always writes a new one just as you tick off the last one. Above all, as Jane will tell you, read poetry. Jane, by the way, is a much nicer person than me. I'll be the bad cop for much of this project, chivvying and poking you to push yourself further and confront unpleasant truths. She'll be right along with soothing advice whenever I offend you.

We'll help you approach your own writing in such a way that you aren't bowled over by its little disappointments, nor by its little successes. We might also help you to redefine success, and to use poetry in a way that bleeds into every minute of your day. For us, poetry is a map to navigate by, a tool to use in tackling daily dilemmas. It's a way of sharing the experiences that go beyond small talk, and exploring the places that hurt, or shine, or sing.

That's why we called this project *How to be a Poet*. Come on in.

CHAPTER TWO
How to Read Widely, and Why it Matters

We've said it loud and clear and in large letters at the very start of proceedings: Read Poetry. Read, for good poetry can never be written without first reading good poetry widely.

One thing heard far too frequently by creative writing tutors in workshops or mentoring sessions is the plaintive cry of *'Oh, of course I don't read other people's poetry in case it influences my own'*. Yet this is *exactly* why you should be reading poetry other than your own.

What results from the kind of mono-cultural and self-informed diet of poetry, where the only poetry being read by the poet is their own, is a thin gruel of a poem which an editor will always spot immediately. Like a wonky bicycle wheel, it is doomed forever to be out of kilter and lacking balance; it is fundamentally flawed. Without fail, these poems will display a lack of craft and a lack of awareness of how hard each line and every word must work to earn its place. It's okay to write these kind of poems to get started, but a good poet is one who strives to move on and to write better, and seeks to take up an apprenticeship with the master craftspersons of their trade.

Can you imagine a great artist who never looks at other art, or the great musician who never listens to any other music, lest it influence their own 'style'?

Far from it – great artists and musicians will always first find and expose themselves to a wide palette of inspiration and influences, and in the early stages of discovering their own styles, will emulate, learn from and then ultimately grow up and beyond the various influences they absorb. The more influences (and the wider the sources of those influences) you take on board, the richer and more adventurous your own writing will be. Learn from the best. Reading poetry widely gives us a chance to ask *what* works, and *how*. It allows us to take a poem apart and see the moving parts to understand the techniques, approaches, form and language at work and get an idea of how it all adds up. That is why our one major piece of advice, alongside writing the thing, and finishing the thing, is that you *must* read, and read widely and voraciously.

Read poems from your contemporaries and gain an understanding of what the current poetry landscape looks like. Who is writing now, what do they write about, and how? You don't need to feel you have to copy or replicate the styles and approaches they have, but you should think about where your place is on this landscape, and which kind of approaches speak to you most directly.

Read also great and classic poems from across time and place, and from cultures and languages other than your own. Read Li Bai and Hafez and Sappho as well as Blake and Keats and Dickinson. Modern poetry in translation, and indeed the superb magazine *Modern Poetry in Translation*, can open doors to some incredible poetry and give you not just a local view of poetry, but a fully global and contemporary one. The widest range of influences will ensure that no one single style or voice becomes a dominant inspiration in your work.

In enjoying and discovering poetry, also allow yourself to like and dislike things. It is completely permissible to dislike a poem, or find that you don't enjoy a particular poet's style or approach. You should never feel that you 'have to' like a poem, or that you have failed if you don't 'get it'. So long as you always interrogate this reaction, work at it; find out perhaps that a poem *does* work, but is complex and rewards being poked and prodded and pondered over. Or perhaps you will discover that, for all its interesting acute angles, you and the poem still don't quite get along, but you know why and will come to understand something of yourself and how *you* want to write by this. These conscious moments of realisation as to why something doesn't quite work for you are just as valuable as the ones where a poem will come to you one day, make itself at home and worm its way into your thoughts and become a part of your daily living and being.

As a publisher, I should at this point declare that I have a professional interest in you reading (and buying) poetry. But I also recognise that not only is there a mind-boggling amount of poetry out there to choose from, but it can be expensive and that many of us lack the funds to buy as many books as we might like to. Libraries, where we remain fortunate enough to still have them, can be invaluable, and our borrowing helps them to stay open. Though not all will have extensive poetry collections, there are some notable exceptions and enthusiastic, poetry-loving librarians out there. If you're lucky enough to be near the Poetry Library at the Southbank Centre in London, it's free to join and there is an embarrassment of poetry riches in its collections – many of which (non-Londoners, visiting for the day, take note) can even be borrowed and posted back.

Other ways to read poetry on a shoestring or non-existent budget is to browse the wealth of resources provided by the Poetry Foundation. Their website features poems, recordings, articles, interviews and much more; the quality of the work you will encounter is guaranteed to be high, and their overview of poetry's contemporary and modern landscapes is fairly comprehensive. And if you're looking for an excellent introduction to contemporary and modern poetry, but are limited in funds and bedazzled by the plethora of possible books to buy, investing in a copy of the *Staying Alive* anthology from Bloodaxe Books, with its myriad of poets, themes, forms and styles, is a really sound place to begin. And you can't go far wrong with the subsequent anthologies *Being Alive* and *Being Human*, either.

One last thing: poetry needs Good Readers. Most of us are happy to go to the Tate without feeling a need to become a sculptor, and few members of any theatre's audience are there because they are aspiring actors – yet each healthy-sized audience makes sure that theatres can continue to be viable, that galleries remain open and stage new exhibitions to throngs of appreciative visitors. If ever an art form needed more audience and appreciators rather than simply more participants, it is certainly poetry. Be an active participant wherever you can, not just a passive contributor.

In the following chapter, let's be Good Readers and put this into practice. Let's also think about what it would mean to 'read like a poet', as Jo continues on this topic and asks you to read a favourite poem of hers very closely, with forensic care.

CHAPTER THREE
On Reading

Let me also reinforce the points from Jane's previous chapter and start with a bald, clear statement. **To write poetry well, you must read poetry.** Reading other people's poetry is the best way to improve your own work. If you take nothing else from this book, believe this.

Some poets see reading as a pursuit entirely separate from their writing – a distraction even. But those who are interested only in their *own* poetry, and not in poetry full stop, often produce work which is self-indulgent and doesn't interest others. Reading is a way of understanding the poetry culture you're part of, its current preoccupations and clichés. It's also a labour-saving device. If you read attentively, every poem you read will teach you as much as three or four painful experiments in drafting.

Note that word 'attentively'. In the ordinary way of reading we skim over the odd word, and take away a general mood or feeling. Reading as a writer requires a closer look at the work in hand. The process needn't be painful nor spoil your pleasure, but you can read poetry in the same way that a painter looks at paintings in a gallery. The painter notes the overall effect first, like any intelligent viewer, but then interrogates the work a little to see what techniques have been used to create it.

Recently I taught a class who all agreed that a particular piece of writing was clichéd and unimaginative. Okay, I said – but which specific *part* of it makes you feel that? The responses varied but all were vague; 'Oh, just all of it' or 'well, it's just old-fashioned isn't it?' I kept bringing them back to the page – 'Yes, but WHERE is it old fashioned? Which words, which turns of phrase, which rhymes are old fashioned?' You can't avoid those effects until you identify them.

That's the secret and the purpose of reading poetry carefully. Poetry, after all, is just marks on a page. Whatever effect a poem has on you is achieved by the placement of words, line breaks and punctuation marks. Whether you find it trite or vivid or dynamic, you can look closely at it to find out exactly what is creating that effect.

I'll talk more about that below, with an example. But where will you find the reading material on which to practice these skills? The classics of world poetry are easy to find in bookshops and libraries, and are very often free as eBooks. You also need to consume current work in reputable journals, collections and web sites. For the purposes of this chapter, 'current work' doesn't mean the drafts of your peers (though you will read those too, I hope), nor the work found on those websites that accept all poems without discrimination.

Poetry journals come and go, but there are a few big names that remain constant. You don't have to subscribe to read them. Most can be bought as a single issue, and in fact buying three single issues of different magazines will give you a better cross section of poetry culture than subscribing to a single one. You can also sample some journals online. *Poetry Review* is the UK flagship, publishing high-end literary poetry. You might enjoy *Magma, Rialto, Poetry London, Ambit* or *Under the Radar* (published, we must declare, by Nine Arches Press). The American journal *Rattle* is full of gems and offers a digital subscription. The US flagship journal *POETRY* is stellar and offers a wide range of styles. As Jane has mentioned, the Poetry Foundation has a great range of poems and essays online, but their free app for smartphones is the single best source I have found for poetry, throwing up random classics or new discoveries while you are waiting for a train.

If you don't like the style of a particular publication – or if you feel it goes right over your head – that is fine. Some of the most esteemed poetry journals contain work that is technically splendid but feels no need to actually say something. One particularly high-end periodical leaves me entirely cold; as a workshopper of mine once said 'It's clever – but it's nothing *but* clever.' If it leaves you cold, find out why by reading it closely but don't beat yourself up about it. You're allowed to dislike even the greatest literary effort, with no shame, but try to pinpoint what it is that makes you dislike it.

All poetry presses are small presses. It's good (and not entirely selfless) to support them by buying books. If you find a poet whose work you love, look at other titles from the same publisher. Seren, Bloodaxe, Carcanet, Cape and Picador are the main poetry imprints but there are many others. Arc specialise in translations, Smokestack in radical or left-wing poetry, Longbarrow in poets of the landscape around Sheffield. There are many other niche publishers in the rich ecology of letters. At the time of writing, Kindle and other eBooks are not the best way to read poetry because they can disrupt the format. Poetry is a visual format – it matters how it looks on the page – so it's best to see it on a page or a larger screen.

Online sources are important, but not all are equal. Anyone can set up a website and some of them are a ragbag of poems accepted by an editor with little discrimination. Good online sources include Josephine Corcoran's *And Other Poems*, Anthony Wilson's archive of *Lifesaving Poems, The Clearing, BODY* and *Angle*. The Poetry Library website has a list of current online journals.

Read poets whose style is unfamiliar and perhaps even unattractive to you. Read poets of a different nationality or background, poets of different centuries, and read poets of a different gender to your own. Male readers, please trust us on this. Research including our own confirms that most men read three or four times as many books by male poets as they do by women. There is an astonishing bias towards men in some of the best-respected newspapers and journals. Poetry after all can be a window into the wider world – you waste much of its potential to illuminate if you use it only as a mirror. We should challenge ourselves constantly in our reading.

Above all, though, read for pleasure and curiosity. Don't feel guilty if your reading takes you far from poetry for a while. In your reading as in your daily life, nothing is wasted. Recently I've been reading about Lady Jane Grey, the Rwandan genocide, wild swimming in Wales, Marcus Aurelius, the Jarrow March and how to write a knitting pattern. Every one of them provoked thoughts that may yet surface in a poem.

William Carlos Williams called a poem 'a small (or large) machine made of words.' Poetry is machinery, not magic and we can understand its workings as well as a car mechanic can understand an engine. Let's have a look at a single poem, and consider how close reading might give us access to more of its meanings. This one is from Kate Clanchy's 1996 Forward Prize-winning collection *Slattern*:

Patagonia　　Kate Clanchy

I said *perhaps Patagonia,* and pictured
a peninsula, wide enough
for a couple of ladderback chairs
to wobble on at high tide. I thought

of us in breathless cold, facing
a horizon round as a coin, looped
in a cat's cradle strung by gulls
from sea to sun. I planned to wait

till the waves had bored themselves
to sleep, till the last clinging barnacles,
growing worried in the hush, had
paddled off in tiny coracles, till

those restless birds, your actor's hands,
had dropped slack into your lap,
until you'd turned, at last, to me.
When I spoke of Patagonia, I meant

skies all empty aching blue. I meant
years. I meant all of them with you.

First question: did you like it? Second question: do you understand it? If you feel that some of its meaning eludes you on the first reading, don't stress about that too much. Very often people who don't 'get' poetry are in the habit of reading fiction. They expect a narrative, a story, a conclusion of some sort. Poetry isn't usually set up to provide a neat ending. It leaves us to do a little contemplation at the end, weighing the content of the poem against our own experience. Those who get anxious about their failure to 'understand' poetry, and who feel excluded and foolish when they read it, are perhaps looking for a kind of completeness which poetry doesn't pretend to provide. On the other hand, if a poem remains entirely obscure, that's a failing of the writer and not the reader.

In this poem by Kate Clanchy there's a lot of stuff missing, and it is all the better for it. In poetry every mark on the page matters, including the ones that aren't there. To start with, there are no speech marks around the only bit of reported speech in this poem – 'perhaps Patagonia'. In modern poetry, italics generally do the job of inverted commas to signify the spoken word.

Nor is there any information about who is speaking (beyond 'I') or to whom. It's unnecessary, because we guess from the last line that it's a lover. If the poet had made that clear earlier, the last line wouldn't have such a punch. Also absent is any explanation of where and in what circumstances this conversation takes place. That doesn't matter because the poem is not really about the conversation. The conversation is only what Richard Hugo calls 'the initiating subject', the incident or object that gives the poet a starting point. It was important enough to get Clanchy thinking, but she uses it to *stand for something* in the poem. That is key to many successful poems – an object, a moment, a throwaway phrase which represents something larger than itself.

From that first phrase, the poem pans out straight away into a broad vision of a possible future in Patagonia. The physical description is all about that imagined place, and it is imagined with all the precision of a longed-for future. They're not just chairs but ladderback chairs, and they wobble. It's not just a narrow peninsula, but a spit 'wide enough for two' which shows us what hopes are being projected onto it. This is a fresh, wide outdoor scene: a horizon is only 'round as a coin' when you can see all of it, and we have gulls, waves, barnacles, a tide, sun and sea. The cold is 'breathless', taking it right into the body. Though the title suggests that the poem is about Patagonia, again that word *stands for* something – a faraway place at the end of the world, the sort of place that we fantasise about going to but which remains a dream for most of us.

At the end of the reverie, returning to the person she or he is speaking to, the narrator stays in that tidal register of language. The lover's hands are like birds, they drop 'slack' like the sluggish water between tides. (Incidentally, if you don't see rhyme in this poem, look again at the sounds which echo in each stanza: I/ wide/ high/ tide, then us/ strung/ gulls/ sun, then barnacles/ coracles, then actor/ slack/ lap/ last and finally, strongest chime of all in blue/ you). I used to read this poem as a straightforward declaration of love – 'I meant years. I meant all of them with you.' Aaah, how romantic. Nowadays I read the gaps as well as the words, and hear what else is missing – the lover's response. The poet and broadcaster Ian McMillan likes to ask poets which word is at the centre of a particular poem: in this case it might be 'perhaps'. The skies are not a dizzying or bright blue but an 'empty, aching blue'. Almost every line break creates a tiny moment of anxiety – 'I pictured….' what? 'I thought…' what? 'Till….' till what? The waves are bored, the barnacles are clinging and worried. So, I think, is the narrator – every stanza break is tense, emphasising 'I thought' or 'I planned' or 'I meant'. It sounds like a sad reappraisal, and the three-times reiterated 'I meant' like a defensive explanation after the event. Every word counts; every word signifies mood. The poet could make the lover's hands quick as fish, or light as sea birds; but no, they are 'actor's hands' and they drop slack into his lap. He turns 'at last' to the speaker, as if he hasn't wanted to. And what will he say? That's for the writer to know, and the reader to surmise.

Reading a poem closely like this shouldn't be a chore, but a small-scale excavation to find out what lies beneath the immediate surface. It gives vital insight into another writer's practice, and hopefully into your own. Like Jane, I also occasionally meet people who say that they don't read other poets because they 'don't want to be influenced.' This is foolishness. We are constantly influenced by everything around us, from the news headlines to the latest style of Nordic thriller. Yes, you will be influenced by reading others' poetry and yes, you may briefly sound like a bad version of Kate Clanchy or Kei Miller after reading their poems. But you will absorb, evolve and move on.

This is not 'being influenced' but learning. Your own readers will eventually do the same, taking from your poems small lessons which feed into the great cycle of cultural change. As you go on reading, you will find out which lessons are relevant to you, and which have no resonance. You will learn from each poem something about rhythm, structure or human behaviour, but ultimately you can only write like yourself. That is your curse and your blessing.

CHAPTER FOUR
On Listening
by Jonathan Davidson

In his essay 'The Poet's Point of View' (1966), the poet Basil Bunting said:

> 'Reading in silence is the source of half the misconceptions that have caused the public to distrust poetry.'

It is a strange way to experience our art, that is true. If we were composers (and we are) then we would scarcely feel satisfied until we had heard our work aloud, either tinkling the ivories ourselves or sitting back and letting our local orchestra or busker belt it out. Music can be experienced in manuscript form, but it was made to be enjoyed aloud. The same is true of poetry. And that which is made of sound must be heard, which is where listening comes in.

Listening is a skill and to hone this skill we are going to have to read less and listen more. Although text of some form has been going for quite a while and may even catch on, the sound of a human voice uttering words came first. And for most of us, words spoken or sung came early in life, which is why we still like to see the face of the speaker, to echo how we watched intently, as infants, the face of our mother or father. To appreciate the best poetry we need to go back to something of that formative relationship, to be watching even as the invisible words pour forth. Just as we did then, we will listen (and look) for shapes and patterns.

Poetry pleases the ear. Its sound structure both 'locks in place' *and* releases the sense of the poem. Prose may make its own functional music and song takes meaning in its arms and dances with it, but poetry knows that it is the setting and shifting of shapes and patterns that will allow the light to shine through the silence. The silence. Every sliver of sound we utter is placed into the silence. Think of the silence as thinking time. However gorgeous the deftly taken line-endings or cascade of consonants, in the silence lies the understanding.

If we are to understand poetry by listening, it needs to be spoken by someone. Sometimes the poet is good at this, although they are often hampered by knowing the work too well. We can do no better than have a novice reader who has had a couple of run-throughs and reads the poem as it is written, blending the sense and the structure and taking Hamlet's advice to the Players. And, if all else fails, we can always speak poems to ourselves, privately or to friends and family. Of course our attention will be split between speaking and listening, but there are lessons to be learned from feeling the sounds leave the mouth. Ideally this should be done from memory, but life is short and (some) poems are long, so reading is an option.

The important thing is that we *hear* poetry. If we hear it we begin to understand how it places itself in the silence, how it is poetry and *not* public announcement or private speech. And if that is known, if we develop an ear as listeners, then those who choose to go on to make poems may also develop an ear as poets. It will take some study. It will take some practice. But having developed an ear for poetry the rest is easy, secure in the knowledge that we are making work that will sound right, whether *we* are speaking it or a passing stranger. Poets, put down your megaphones and put away your dictionaries. Now listen.

Jonathan Davidson has read poetry – or had it read to him – for many years, beginning with a book called *Poems* by Walter de la Mere in 1965. Since then he has heard poetry read by poets and performers at several thousand live events, some of which he was involved in organising. His collection of essays, *On Poetry – Jonathan Davidson*, about his experience of poetry as a reader and listener, is published by Smith|Doorstop in Spring 2018.

CHAPTER FIVE
How to Learn from Art and Artists

'Always go a little further into the water than you feel you're capable of being in. Go a little bit out of your depth, and when you don't feel that your feet are quite touching the bottom, you're just about in the right place to do something exciting.' – David Bowie

In my previous chapter, I wrote about reading widely. I also want to write about the importance of being a cultural omnivore and looking beyond your own realm of specialism as a poet to what we can also learn from other artists. What we're talking about here is cross-pollination between art forms and approaches – and how it can be of value to your own perspectives on writing.

When I left school I took a year to go and study an art foundation course at my local college; I wasn't particularly great at art, but I did make some wobbly pots, completed some passable paintings, and experienced things that opened the doors for me in lots of other ways. We went on trips all over the place, turned up late and worked late, created things that went terribly wrong, made and broke friendships and were trusted to find and make our own way, for better or for worse. We also learnt how to take our craft seriously; we were taught to think about scale and starting points, and how to study the techniques of other artists. Magpie-eyed, we mixed high and popular culture, learned to 'get our eye in' and look at things afresh, take oblique angles, seek parallels, points of contact and points of reference.

I'm not suggesting that you pack it all in now, forget writing poetry and hurry off to sign up for your nearest art course, but I hope that this illustrates how our cultural commonwealth can be a resource of ideas and inspiration, and provide us with sage advice and manifestos for making. Keeping our wider creative radar tuned-in can help us to be fully-fledged not just as writers but as creative beings.

Culture isn't just in galleries and museums, or on arts courses or programmes of study. It's in our cinemas and record shops, in small venues and on stage, on our streets, in daily conversations and daily breaking of bread, outdoors in the landscape, on TV and online or anywhere else it can find you.

Art and culture is invaluable to the writer because we can learn so much from it about the minds' eye (or even the minds' ear, if we're talking about music) and how to stimulate and appeal to it.

For instance, let's think for a moment about how film and television teaches us to think about detail, particularly the kind of subtle detail which is about imagination and 'showing' rather than 'telling' (we'll come back to this topic later on). The very best films or TV work beyond the screen, involving our own imagination and playing with our attention, making active participants of the viewer. Through visual motifs and the power of image and metaphor, we are able to approach and reflect in parallel on the 'big themes' of human existence. What can a writer take away from this? That metaphors, similes, motifs and images allow us to find a subtle, sideways approach to the big, life-and-death matters of the universe which are, in their own right, just too vast to set down on the table in front of your audience like an immovable monolith. And that by involving and innately trusting your reader (viewer/audience) to take the leap with you, you will not only involve them imaginatively in what you're doing, but reward them for bringing their own imagination to the table.

Also, the way in which artists think about what they make, their advice, their manifestos and the ideas they propose can help motivate and shape our work as poets and writers, too. The Bowie quote at the start of this article is a useful provocation for creativity, putting exactly into words that complicated *out of my depth / frankly terrified / rather excited* feeling we get when we create something that might actually be close to our best work. It also touches on how we should learn to instinctively go with this reaction, and come to know and trust where it is taking us if we want to get out of our comfort zones and make work that consistently challenges and changes us.

There's a reason that I put certain music on when I'm trying and failing to write; I find that it provides me motivation and reminds me why I want to write in the first place, where I'm coming from and what I want to say. In music, we will often find the soundtrack to bring our own imaginings and visualisations to. When writing about Coventry, the city I was born in, I went back to The Specials' debut album to get the right atmosphere, and found the sensation of a certain place in time coming to me vividly. I responded by writing not about the music itself, but the shared connections I have with it in a physical place, the city's people and its story. What would be your own writing soundtrack? And what might you write if you were to listen to a piece of experimental electronica, grime, or a choral piece? This is to say nothing of form, rhythm, sound and so much more that music can teach us about. Or the way that a perfectly placed punch-line in comedy teaches us about the importance of timing. And what a pleasure it is to learn techniques and ideas through things we can enjoy participating in hearing, seeing, laughing at, feeling…

So do read widely, yes, and read beyond poetry. But also be active in finding inspiration and approaches within all that art and culture can offer you. Try thinking like a dancer about the rhythms of your poetry – where will you next put your foot, and how will this matter? Think like an architect as you build the stanzas or rooms of your poems. Raid art's make-up bag and come up wearing some kind of 'brand new drag', if it helps you to get closer to what you need to say and how it needs to be said. Look at the poem's scene through a view-finder – get the distinct angle, perhaps even find your own Fibonacci spiral in an unlikely place.

CHAPTER SIX
On Looking

'I see no more than you, but I have trained myself to notice what I see.' – Sherlock Holmes, in Conan Doyle's *The Adventure of the Blanched Soldier*

I'm trying to say something in this chapter which is important to me, and I am confronted with two problems. I don't quite know what it is I want to say, and I don't quite know how to say it. I will only find out what I have to say by trying to say it – and I will only find out how to say it, by repeatedly getting it wrong. Frankly, it's a pain in the neck.

It's also the central process of writing poetry. Practical advice is easy to give – how to deal with rejection, how to get the most benefit from reading poetry, and so on. We'll get to that, and there is a very practical exercise at the end of this chapter. But let's not confuse technique or ambition with the real skills and pleasures of poetry; the endless wrangling with what we see, what we think, and how to say it so that others might see it too.

The best poetry is at once very private and very public. Take a poem like Louis MacNeice's 'Snow' for instance, one that describes a moment in MacNeice's life. I didn't share that moment with him, but I know what he means about the 'drunkenness of things being various'. That sense of intoxicating variety hadn't occurred to me before reading 'Snow', but ever since I did it's been a part of my world view. I borrow MacNeice's insight, as you might borrow mine from another poem. It's a conversation that carries on even after death.

'Being a poet' isn't about knowing how many lines there are in a pantoum, or getting published in *Poetry Review*. It's a way of seeing, and you can learn it. What all good poets have in common is an appetite for looking. They notice things, and communicate in a way that makes the reader notice them too. Poets (like many other artists) develop a habit of paying close attention. If you notice everything around you – how a particular person speaks, how light falls on the water, what your own reaction is to a news story, how people behave in a pub fight or at a petrol station – then you have the raw material for poetry.

After that, everything is selection. This is a whole different can of worms, which we'll address worm by worm in the next chapters. Select the right words, and discard the wrong ones. Work out as you write exactly what it is you're trying to say, and what the best way to express it is. What could be simpler? Almost anything. You'll never master it completely but you can hope to do it better each time. In the old sense of the word, writing a poem is a meditation – what my dictionary explains as 'the act of thinking about something carefully, calmly, seriously, and for some time, or an instance of such thinking'.

✐ *Top Tips*

Here's an exercise to develop that habit of looking; the hardest, simplest and best I've ever devised. Go outside and select one square metre of ground (one yard, if you're feeling Imperial). It doesn't have to be a particularly interesting metre of ground. Now: stand or sit in your metre of ground and write down everything you notice about it, without judgment. Simply describe. The fallen leaves are not 'melancholy', they are 'wet' or 'brown' or 'one of them is split across the middle'. The paving stones may have a texture like fabric; there may be a cigarette butt or a snail shell in the middle of one. There may be a footprint. What can you hear, smell, taste? Are you feeling foolish and thinking this is a waste of time? It's an exercise in noticing, and it's a palate cleanser for the harder work of writing about things that matter to you; but if you are just paying attention, then you are learning the most important lesson about How to Be a Poet.

CHAPTER SEVEN
How to Start a Poem

Where does the poem begin? It's a very good question.

I'd wager that most good poems have their roots firmly in your memory and imagination long before the words themselves ever make their way onto the page. Even before you realise it, the first inklings of a poem are there, lodged amongst ideas that interest, excite or trouble you, awaiting the catalytic moment and the right handful of words that will bring it into being.

Sometimes, the poem-in-waiting is released by a throwaway phrase we hear in a crowd, an image that comes to mind when we're about to go to sleep, or a memory that comes back to us when we take a short cut through a place we used to know. The right line or phrase might rise to the surface, and bring together a number of previously unconnected thoughts and designs. Like bacteria on a petri dish, it is sometimes the introduction of the germ of an idea to the right environmental conditions that will help a poem find its place to flourish.

There are no secret tricks for getting a poem out and onto the page, but you will, as your confidence and experience as a poet grows, learn to trust your writing habits and know how to follow up the scent of a good poem, doggedly. There will also be times when it is something more formal – an exercise, a form or structure, or an over-arching concept, that will help a poem to be realised and come alive. Poetry is part alchemy, part practical formula. It is in these combinations that we find new things happening; somewhere between happenstance and constrictions, the rule-making and rule-breaking.

I was recently talking to a mentee about the process of writing poems and they confessed they were looking forward to the time when, like 'all the proper poets' they would 'no longer struggle to start a poem'. I admitted to them (and I hope that it reassuring in a way to know this, rather than disheartening) that the anxiety of the blank page and how to get the poem started never really goes away, whatever stage a writer is at, and that even the most successful poets you can think of will still wrestle with starting, sustaining and writing a poem. There will always be times when a poem is difficult to coax out, and I encouraged them to not to think that the once you are a 'proper poet' (a false distinction we use when we are yet to step fully into our own authority as writers) it all suddenly becomes easy and you no longer experience this struggle to create. All we can learn is how to manage the difficulties of the process so they do not become limiting – and to both control and embrace the forces which may otherwise stop us writing altogether, and put them to good work in serving the poem.

How, then, do we combine good writing habits with this complicated mix of discipline and inspiration? How do we make time for these two unlikely companions to find each other on good terms and help a poem to find its beginning?

Our headful of ideas can only start to take shape if you can give them the necessary page space, writing space and time to do so. However, the reality is that we all lead busy, noisy lives. We are interrupted by the demands of our everyday business, we bend to the siren call of our emails and notifications, we have work to do and lives often full of unplanned diversions, and we are bound by the time we need to give to others and to ourselves to keep it all together. None of us here are frilly-shirted scribes in wistful towers, biding our time until the muse finds us, and it is completely fine to admit to this.

With this in mind, let's explore some tips on how we ensure that, even in the midst of our busy lives, we can still create small pockets of time to write in, and suggest some ways in which you can get poems jump-started…

The regular act of writing and of writing in small but steady amounts will be your companion. Don't worry at the early stages about whether it's any good. It's too early to tell. Write long, and be prepared to sift the glimmer of promising treasure from the note-form poems and scrawled ideas. Regular writing does not have to be every day, or follow any form of regimented programme of 'enforced' writing time. Follow what feels right and natural for you – it might be setting aside the last day of every month as a writing day, for instance.

Get your attention back. If you find social media or the online world in general a massive distraction, delete your apps, even just for a few hours, or only use social media between certain hours. Take away the temptation and make sure you reduce the chance for updates and notifications to interrupt you as you reclaim your writing and thinking time. Put an out-of-office or vacation message on your email for a day or two so you won't feel the knee-jerk necessity to respond to things immediately.

If you only have limited time to write, work with this rather than against it. Not many of us have the luxury of days at a time to give to writing, or even hours, so don't feel frustrated by lack of time and let this stop you writing. There is a myth that abounds that all great poetry has to be written on a workshop, retreat, or an MA Creative Writing course, or by spending days and days at a time in writing – whilst these can be useful, they can also be unrealistic at this stage, when all you really need to do is sit down somewhere with your words when you can. I didn't realise I'd written a complete collection of poems until someone made me sit down and look at the ten years' worth of poems I had gradually been accruing. Don't let the illusion of waiting for 'special writing time' – ring-fenced and just out of reach – stop you from writing. Follow your urges, write when you can and when you have something to say.

Create small bursts of time for writing if that is all you have – anything from a regular ten minutes to an hour. Get up early, or if you're a night-owl, add half an hour onto the day for writing. Keep a diary and develop a habit for writing regularly even if it's nothing like poetry yet – all writing is good writing practice, so don't worry if you're not producing poems but just notes, sketches and ideas, long screeds that aren't yet quite forming themselves. You can come back at a later stage. Rescue the time that you normally spend reading the papers on the train or waiting for the potatoes to boil, or spend online doing nothing in particular.

Keep everything you write, and come back to it when you are able to set aside some concentrated time for redrafting. Not all of this writing will be good or even necessary, but amongst it you may find the spark you are looking for. Book an afternoon out to your writing when you feel ready to get your notes in order (just as you'd book some time out to go the dentists, but hopefully more enjoyable). Make sure you have a few hours to follow where the threads of where your writing wants to go. Use this time to redraft as well as writing new things. You will find that having time to redraft not only helps to continually sharpen poems (and your editorial instincts), but will nourish your creative imagination; you are more likely to be better attuned to producing further new writing in this mindset.

Value time and space to simply *think* about things. Spend time not writing but thinking and even just doing other things that leave the mind free to wander; crafts, physical activity, chores. I ruminate on poems long before I ever write them, even if I don't actively realise this is what I'm doing. I think about them when I'm cooking, or walking the dog or daydreaming on the train. I turn ideas over and over, and find some of the best lines will rise up out of nowhere and come to me when I'm occupied in something else. Things will come back to me, years after I first thought about them, finally finding their right moment in the spotlight.

Note down those little ideas that drop into your head, and try not to lose them – pop them on your phone or in a notebook. The seeds of an idea are so valuable and often the beginnings of something much larger that you can come back to when you've more time to give to them. I find that when I note down odd lines, and finally return to them, they will surprise me by taking off in unexpected directions. It's as if in noting it down, you allow something to quietly take root. Offline, you brain is still turning the idea over even if you're not fully conscious of it. Writing it *makes* it real.

Give yourself permission to write anything. Don't think at this stage about writing a poem or doing anything except putting a pen to paper. If writing is like exercising a muscle (the imagination), sometimes a more extended warm up is necessary. No one is going to ask to see your notes, any more than they'd want to watch athletes limbering up for an hour before a marathon, so don't fret if nothing that appears to be a poem has emerged to begin with.

Give yourself permission to write long and to write badly, to write nonsense, and for now, especially if you're finding getting started difficult, just to write. Write non-stop and automatically for a few minutes, even if it means writing one sentence or word again and again until you can break out of it and make a dash for something new to say.

Change the scene, change the tempo. If writing in a quiet space is just too intimidating and the pressure of using the time to write is making it, counter-intuitively, difficult to write, don't fret. This is a common reaction to having all that valuable time to write and then finding yourself under pressure to fulfil the promise of it all. If you can, write somewhere different for a change, like a noisy and bustling cafe. Or if this doesn't work for you or isn't possible, try writing in your usual space to music or sounds, changing the style and tempo of the music to see how this might change the atmosphere and the way you write. Most importantly, take the pressure off – it's not a coursework assignment, so don't demand so much of yourself that it becomes a barrier to actually getting words down on paper.

Don't demand or set targets of writing a poem good enough for this, or publishable enough for that – just aim, in the words of Samuel Beckett, *to fail better* than last time. Aim simply to write. And if it's not working, go and do something else.

Remember: There is no single right way to write. There is no special writer's secret that will make a poem happen more easily or help future ones through their messy and difficult stages more quickly. Find what works for you, and don't worry if the way you write or what you find to be the most productive and positive methods doesn't fit with what seems to be the accepted narrative of writerly success. Everyone will find ways that are differently productive. Many are free or of low cost, so don't feel you also have to invest vast sums of money in writing retreats, workshops or one-to-one mentoring to be successful. These can of course be useful and valuable at certain stages, but no more useful or vital than the act of writing itself in the first instance, and won't help if you're not already reading poetry widely, engaging with poetry and learning about the techniques that will enable you to challenge yourself as a writer.

Be prepared that there will be times when writing is an excruciating, difficult business, when you feel like you have nothing to say, or no way of saying it. Your dictionary will feel dry of words, no ideas will present themselves. **It is okay to not write, too.**

And there will be times when the blank page will taunt you, and times when you fail and when you will give in. There will be disheartening times when you experience writer's block, and may even decide to no longer write at all.

Let's talk about those experiences in my next chapter.

✍ Top Tips

Workshop exercises and writing prompts can be a good way to get your writing kick-started and to write things you may not have expected to write. It can give permission to the mind to try something out new within the framework of an exercise, and liberate the imagination to go off-piste and off-plan.

Why not try some of these quick writing prompts and exercises to get a poem started:

Q&A Exercise

Pick one of the following: a mountain, the sea, a hurricane or a wildfire. Write down three questions you'd like to ask them, and then write their replies. Is there a poem in either, or both of these? You can adapt this Q&A to almost anything. Take it outdoors and ask the statues in the park, or indoors, ask the four walls to speak to you. Ask a dead poet or a fictional character for your favourite book or film to speak to you. Lots of possibilities here, but this exercise is also an enjoyable distraction that can produce some unexpected results.

Numbers

There is something about numbers which makes for a satisfying juxtaposition to words and language, and a good trigger for the imagination to take a meander off its more usual patterns and tracks. First, think of a memorable number. A telephone number from long ago, a house you once lived in, a post code. Make this your title. Write the poem that goes with it. You can do the same with a date, either a significant one, or one plucked from thin air. You could even work with OS Map grid references, use a mathematical or even scientific formula. What might emerge from 3.14159, or from $E=MC^2$? Each time, begin with your number as your title. Give yourself twenty minutes and see what can flow from this prompt.

The important thing to remember with any prompt is that you give yourself the freedom to dive in and follow wherever it takes you – and don't think the poem you write has to be *about* the prompt – in fact, the further you can roam from the prompt, the better. In redrafting and writing onwards from your first ideas, allow the idea to run wild and go wherever it needs to. Likewise, poetic form can be a useful way not only to begin a poem but also to stretch yourself. Rather than acting as an imposing constriction, form can be a freeing, liberating and practical agent in your poetry writing – the poet Mona Arshi will have more to say on this in Chapter Eleven.

Some poets will often begin with form, and use it as a way to give shape to their ideas. But why not try this following exercise to take a failing poem and put it through the 'prism' of a poetic form, and see what emerges from the other side:

Form and Breaking the Rules Exercise

Choose a draft poem that is not yet working. Next, select a poetic form, e.g. a sonnet, a sestina, a pantoum, a specular or a ghazal (a very useful list of poetry forms can be found at the Poetry Foundation website if you're seeking inspiration). Redraft the poem by using the frame of the form to restructure and, in effect, rewrite it. Allow yourself in the next draft to break just one rule of the form to make an improvement to your poem.

CHAPTER EIGHT
On the First Draft

'The last time I heard Seamus Heaney speak, he was asked to
define poetry in 3 words. After a long pause he said:
Exact. Truthful. Melodious.'
– Michael Bazzett @mikhailbazharov

Words are a blunt tool with which to tackle our lived experience, but they are what we have. Each of us approaches the blank page or screen with a different package of life stories, attitudes and interests. Each of us has to start somewhere; with a memory, a mood, a global or personal incident.

As you begin to write, remain open to the possibility that the poem isn't about what you thought it was about. Indeed, the thing that first struck you – the way a tree looks in the rain, a perfect goal scored by your favourite striker – is very unlikely to be the real subject of the poem. It probably interested you in the first place because it stands for something that resonates at a deeper level. Richard Hugo, in his book *The Triggering Town*, makes a useful distinction between

> the initiating or triggering subject, which starts the poem or 'causes' the poem to be written, and the real or generated subject, which the poem comes to say or mean, and which is generated or discovered in the poem during the writing.

That first subject jump-starts the poem, but it begins a stream of thought which might take you somewhere else entirely. If you start writing with a particular message in mind and doggedly pursue it, you may end up missing something more subtle and honest. Let go a little, and see where you end up.

My own approach is to start, not with an idea I want to express but with something that strikes me about the physical world, as I suggested in *On Looking*. I don't mean that you should write only about the physical world, so that your poem is about the taste of oranges and not about the joy you felt this morning. I mean that if you do it well, the taste of oranges will stand for joy.

In your case, that physical incident might be, say, the appalling traffic on your way to work. Don't worry how to make it *mean* something. If you noticed it, it meant something. Note down everything about it, concentrating particularly on the five senses. The smell of exhaust fumes, the endlessly repeated view of a single person in a car with the occasional variation of a child or a dog in the back, the sign that says THIS ROUNDABOUT IS SPONSORED BY AMIR'S DOUGHNUTS. Get it all down.

Stay focused on the physical, avoiding lyrical interpretations or florid descriptions. Do not say, for instance, that 'there is a mournful halo of mist over the motorway; melancholy swirls of fog'. Stick to what you actually see and feel. It's misty. Some of the cars have their fog lights on. The air feels metallic and wet. Be specific too. Was it the Tinsley bypass or the turn-off for Little Gidding? Was it a Volvo or a Vauxhall that you saw? Format doesn't matter here. Do not worry about rhymes, or strain to make wise observations. No-one is looking over your shoulder. Just observe.

At this stage, gag the personal devil who tells you that your phrases are too crazy or too orthodox – that you should *definitely* write a sonnet or villanelle – that you must know precisely What Your Poem is About. Instead, keep hold of the opportunity to surprise yourself. Don't worry about surprising or impressing the reader: as yet, there is no reader. Let everything spill on to the page without filtering or over-thinking. Don't get it right, get it written. This more or less ordered jumble is your raw material. There will be plenty of editing and refining in the days to come.

Your method may be different from mine. You might start by drawing a mind map or annotating a *New Scientist* article, but I find that building from the bottom up like this gives a firm foundation on which you can stand some very delicate and subtle ideas. I feel increasingly that the poet's job is to get out of the damn way of the poem, and let it come through. In the first stages, at any rate, trust your subconscious to spot that which is of real importance, and only later bring wordcraft into play.

Whatever your notes look like, you have got something on the page. Have a cup of tea. Come back to your notes, congratulate yourself for having got this far, and get to work. These first steps are a repeated sorting or filtering processes. Terry Pratchett said that 'The first draft is you telling yourself the story,' and subsequently we work out how to communicate our ideas to someone else.

What do you do with that first splurge of notes? Discard first the big, obvious chunks of clutter – the phrases that don't make sense to you any more, the tangent which serves no purpose. Look at the very beginning of your draft. Very often writers do a sort of mental warm-up to get into the right frame of mind. If your first lines are nothing more than you saying 'let me see now, where and when did that interesting thing happen?' then they can be discarded. Your notes on the traffic jam may say 'M6, junction 15 there was a massive tailback. Something spilled on the road, police on the scene. I noticed a man in the car behind me….' You could put a line through all of that, call it TRAFFIC JAM, M6 and start with 'The man in the car behind me….'

From now on, a great deal of your work consists in simple selection. You can undo any changes. For example, the right order of events may not be chronological. Start at the end, or begin with one image that has a powerful impact. Every image you select has an effect on the tone of the poem. Perhaps the man in the car behind you was singing along to the radio at the top of his voice, whilst you were listening to a traffic report about the tailback you were already sitting in. Put that at the centre of your poem and it becomes a piece about his optimism versus your pessimism. If on the other hand the AMIR'S DOUGHNUTS sign turns your mind to creeping commercialism, then your poem changes focus and the singing commuter becomes expendable. If you want to emphasise the mindful pleasure of the moment you might cut out the exhaust fumes, and spotlight the roadside flowers that you noticed as the traffic stood still. To highlight the environmental impact of commuting, you would cut out the singing man and devote a line or two to the squashed badger and the hum of planes overhead. Bit by bit, your choices will start to shape the poem.

Resist settling on a form too early in the process, and absolutely resist setting out with the intention of 'writing a sonnet' or 'writing a ghazal', unless as a training exercise. The relationship between form and subject is organic, and becomes clear in the writing. For instance, the endless repetition of your daily commute might suggest a repeated phrase. The line of traffic could suggest a series of couplets, each dealing with a different car. Look at what you've written so far: are there accidental refrains or internal rhymes you could make use of? Hone in on them. Select and discard, select and discard.

The more poetry you *read*, the better equipped you'll be to make those decisions. As for your readers – don't worry about them too much. At this moment, they don't exist. In your next draft, you will start to think about readers. Right now, the important thing is to work out what you are saying. Don't worry about who you're saying it to.

Have another cup of tea. You're ready for your second draft, which is the most important one.

CHAPTER NINE
How to Recover from a Full Stop

As we talk about drafting, redrafting, and pushing onwards with our writing, let us take a little side-step and talk about something that you may think of variously as not writing, a phobia of the blank page, or writer's block.

I'm not talking here the natural ebb and flow of ideas of my previous chapter, but the stage where you really cannot write at all, and the desire to make a poem has withered. This is when not writing becomes more a serious issue; your writing simply stops completely, not just for weeks or months, but for extended periods of time, and you really can't get it going again, not matter what tricks you try.

There may be a level at which this has deepened from a temporary barrier to writing, into an immovable and definite block. A dreadful combination of terror and a complete lack of confidence may beset you. You will feel defeated. You may not have even written for months, a year maybe, and whatever poetry you read no longer fills you with the joy of possibilities but simply parades all the glittering brilliance you feel you will never come close to, no matter how much you write and how hard you try.

Self-doubt waylays you, and nothing can make the words or ideas come. You try too hard and attempt something intricate and highly stylised (perhaps a sequence of poems or a complex theme) and when this ambitious idea crashes and burns, or the next rejection rolls in, you're ready to give it all up. There are other things you could do with your time, yes? And doesn't dry-stone walling or macramé or cosplay look like an attractive hobby?

Let's stop here for a moment.

Every single successful writer has been here, to the familiar and dispiriting territory of the complete full stop. Don't think for a minute that for a single one of us, writing a poem ever comes easily because we've been doing it for a while now and even had things published. There will be times when writing dries up entirely for us, too. It's important not to despair – this won't last forever. Let me, if I may, reassure with you by telling you about something that happened to me.

I was unfortunate several years ago to be in receipt of some bad advice about my writing – the kind I shouldn't have taken on board, the sort of feedback that isn't constructive. This advice utterly floored me, and I felt the aftershocks of it over several years as I tried and failed to write again. I had yet to fully develop enough confidence and instinct in what I was doing as a writer. I wasn't yet able to step into my own authority as a poet and separate the right kinds of criticism from the wrong, or the positive (and motivating) kind of dissatisfaction with my work from the more destructive sort. The bad advice dogged me whenever I opened a new document on my computer to start writing, or lifted a pen and opened my notebook to sketch out some words towards a poem. *Why*, I thought each time, *would anyone care what I have to say?* The critical voice, peering over my shoulder, taunted *It won't be any good, anyway*. I could barely bring myself to write anymore.

I gave up. For more than three years I wrote very little poetry, and lost faith in almost everything I had ever written previously. This period of not writing only really came to an end with the passage of time, experience and the encouragement of other fellow poets. I'd been reading and editing manuscripts for several years by this time, as well as teaching workshops and mentoring poets – and it was partly this which helped me to rebuild my confidence and stop feeling so fearful of my own writing. I was able to take the first steps in stepping into my own authority as a writer – *I can do this*, I thought, *I can write a reasonable poem, and know what needs fixing when it isn't working*.

47

I was able to step back to re-examine the bad advice I'd been given more carefully, and then to look objectively at my work again, as if I was my own editor. I started taking the poems out once more, trying them out on fellow writers whose opinions I trusted to be challenging but constructive. I slowly regained my faith in my ability and instinct to honestly spot the faults and merits of my own without wanting to tear the whole thing down.

It's important to say that I didn't do this alone. I was tremendously lucky to find other writers who were supportive and gave well-rounded, thoughtful criticism. They didn't hold back and were truthful with me, but the advice they gave was practical, offered solutions, identified faults and bad habits. They did simple but powerful things: inviting me to join workshop groups, giving me space and time and advice generously. And with a little of my confidence rebuilt and some new poems flowing, I was able to pick up where I had left off, and start to write new poems.

This not only gave me the strength to write again, but to write more fearlessly. I learnt to come to terms with and embrace the worries, insecurities and self-doubts that abound and taunt us when we write. We have to pack the bad-critic voices away in order to get the words down on the blank page, but to also know when to put the useful nosy-editor voice to work when we are redrafting and refining our poems.

Writing poetry and making your poetry public in any way is frightening. It is an exposing, risky and hair-raising business. Sometimes, your best writing will feel like one of those dreams where you are walking down the high street naked. I now know that it's okay to feel like this. I feel it, believe it or not, right now as I write this very chapter, and consider the prospect of making it public and putting into print for all to see. I am more at peace with the fact that my insecurities and fears and discomfort about writing will never completely go away, and I've come to realise that you can employ these fears in your writing practice. Use them to help you redraft and edit without fear, to push the poem to be the very best it can be, to be a little more fearless each time.

We have to embrace that discomfort, and accept that it never becomes easier or completely diminishes with time – we must dare to dance toe-to-toe in tango with our terrified selves sometimes, because when we're close to something good, this is how it can feel. Exposing, truthful, dangerous seat-of-your-pants stuff. Push on through this feeling and get it written.

CHAPTER TEN
On the Second Draft

Some people proudly proclaim that they never work on a poem beyond the first draft. 'Oh, I never edit,' they trill. 'I just let the words come from the Muse, and any tampering with them after that is wrong.'

You will notice that I don't call these people poets. They are usually new to poetry. They pride themselves on how little time it takes them to write a poem, and they consider it finished as soon as it hits the page. These are, as we've previously mentioned, the same people who don't read other work because they don't want to be 'influenced'. They should be so lucky. All artists are voracious consumers of their art form, because they want to learn what's out there now, what has happened in the past, what their own work looks like in context. And on the whole, all artists find their first draft, or sketch, or maquette, hopelessly inadequate. It's the stage where you think that you have nothing to say, or you do have something to say but you don't know what it is, or you have something to say but someone said it already. Spare yourself that last one, at least. We don't often find a subject that no-one has covered in the history of literature. Your take on it can still be unique and memorable.

I don't mean that *nobody* gets it right first time. Sometimes one strikes lucky and a more or less finished poem arrives straight away (though as they say, 'the harder I work, the luckier I get.') Nor do I fetishise the poet who weeps over her ninety-seventh draft, sweating blood into the keyboard and trembling over a rhyme for 'artichoke'. Somewhere between the two is a level of effort that will chip the knobbly bits off your first draft and make it more like the shape you are striving for. A poem is a tool for imagining. Drafting is what we do to make it function.

If, as Terry Pratchett said, the first draft is us telling ourselves the story, then subsequent revisions are where you find out how to make it clear to others, where you start a relationship with the imagined reader. The inner critic whom you worked so hard to dodge in the first draft can begin to help you now.

The American teacher of writing, Sol Stein, compared writing to another intimate exchange:

> Sex has to be good for both partners. That is also the key to writing….It has to be a good experience for both partners, the writer and the reader, and it is a source of distress to me to observe how frequently writers ignore the pleasure of their partners.

These are suggestions that you might find useful in getting from first base to second. With your draft in hand, consider whether these steps are of use to this particular poem:

Cut ~~cut cut~~! Take out *every* word that isn't necessary, including 'and' and 'the'. You are not aiming for the stilted, pronoun-free language that some beginners use: 'trees bend in wind, man walks, cars line up in dark alley' etc. This style is common with writers who imagine that contemporary poetry sounds like this, but haven't actually read any. Keep the sense and flow of your sentences – but trim off the superfluous words. It's astonishing how few words are needed to convey large ideas.

You can get rid of most adjectives and adverbs, especially once you've attended to the verbs as I advise overleaf. Remove unnecessary syllables – if something is *rising up* or *falling down*, then the word 'up' or 'down' can be cut. 'Very' and 'suddenly' are almost always unnecessary. The word 'somehow' is a little alarm bell indicating that you should come back to this line and work out *how*. Remove accidental repetition, or beautiful gibberish. The words 'I think' or 'I wonder' are mostly unnecessary, like the Twitter profiles which tell us that 'all opinions expressed are my own'. We know. We know you think it, because you wrote it. You don't need to say *I ask myself, why does this happen?* or *I saw on the news tonight a woman caught by the Houston floods....* As a rule, *Why does this happen?* or *a woman caught by the Houston floods....* will sound punchier.

Be wary of lines which use florid description or make a neat classical reference, but are really there to show how clever you are. The difference between a good poem and a bad one is often ego: the poet couldn't let go of something that made him look intellectual, and is effectively twirling his mustachios at the reader. There's a similar effect when the poet can't let go of something that had personal meaning but which makes no sense to the reader. Above all, remove words that are there only for the rhyme. We can tell.

Poetry consists of the best words in the best order, as Coleridge said. Select and discard, select and replace. Consider syllable counts and rhythm in even the smallest words. Replacing 'but' with 'however' makes the line longer, but might give you a chime with 'seven' in the next line. Word order is important too. Roy Peter Clark in his *Writing Tools* quotes a newspaper article about an aeroplane crash which hit a school. The anxious parents arrive at the school in 'jogging suits, business clothes, housecoats.' Any other order weakens the sentence. Placing 'housecoats' at the end builds the urgency of the situation: parents racing from their homes dressed as they are.

It's at this molecular level that decisions are made about your poem. Rearrange. See what effect each choice has. Use line breaks to reinforce or camouflage those choices.

For a good exercise in editing, try making a found poem. Look at verbatimpoetry.blogspot.co.uk for examples. Use a source like a newspaper article, Facebook post or restaurant menu. You're allowed to cut words but not to add them. It's surprising how much meaning one can squeeze out of a seemingly unpromising text, using only selection and line breaks. I find this a useful exercise for reminding me how little a poet actually needs to do to signpost a reader to the intended meaning.

Every word counts. Once redundant words have been surgically removed, check that you are getting full value out of those that remain. That woman caught by the floods – is she just 'a woman' or can you specify that she is a white woman, a teenager, a matron, a jogger? Is the dog in your poem a greyhound or a Jackapoo? Each one gives better value, signifies something different – and of course, each has a different sound to feed into your rhyme or metre. Don't hesitate to change a small fact if it improves the flow of sense or sound. His name was actually Nigel, but David will make a better rhyme with 'made' in the following line? Feel free to change it. Tiny changes can have vast implications. Consider Auden's edit of his *September 1, 1939*. He famously changed the line 'We must love one another *or* die' to 'We must love one another *and* die'; the whole tone and meaning of the poem changes because of that change.

Adverbs: Underline every one in your draft (stiffly, dizzily, slowly etc.). Writers use adverbs when they don't trust the verb – or worse, when they don't trust the reader. Most of the time a precise verb will do the work on its own. For example, 'cowering fearfully' – is there any other way to cower? See what happens if you cut every word that ends in 'ly', fixing vague verbs as you go along (see below). The poem should start to feel stronger. Adverbs aren't forbidden – nothing is – but they have to serve some purpose.

Verbs: The verb is the engine of the poem. If someone in your poem is 'walking slowly' could they be slouching, limping, stumbling or plodding? A good verb will do the work of two adjectives. Be as physical as you can – perhaps your narrator is not *looking*, but squinting or scrying or scanning. Not waving but drowning.

Abstract nouns are to be hunted down and killed wherever possible. Circle all of them in your first draft. Pain, grief, joy, and above all LOVE may well be at the centre of your poem but oddly, if you deliver them in those words you remove the point of poetry. Your job is not to describe your own feelings, but to make the reader feel them too. This is what the old saw 'show, don't tell' means. If I tell you I'm grieving, you are sympathetic but it makes no impact on you personally. If on the other hand I show you that I see my dead wife's wedding ring on the dresser every morning, you *experience* a sliver of my grief. You feel it in response to the same trigger. As poet EL Doctorow once wrote, 'Good writing is supposed to evoke sensation in the reader; not the fact that it's raining, but the feeling of being rained upon.'

Dots and dashes: punctuation. Every atom of ink on the page serves a purpose. A full stop does something different from a semicolon. A question mark or exclamation mark is an instruction for the reader. These are signposts to help us navigate through the poem. If you get it right, it becomes almost impossible to mistake mood, pace and ultimately meaning. Line breaks are not a substitute for punctuation, so unless you're deliberately aiming for breathlessness you need both. Remember that a stanza doesn't have to be a sentence, or vice versa. Pay attention to your usual patterns of speech. Do you always use short sentences, or long ones with many clauses? Vary your habits to give the poem texture and pace. If you aren't sure about proper use – KEEP READING and learn from other poets.

Adjectives: One is usually enough, and often too many. Very often an early draft is loaded with pairs of them; the *bright yellow* trees, the *soft tabby* cat, the *weeping sullen* child. Treat adjectives as strong medicine and go easy on them. As a broad rule, if it could be the name on a Farrow & Ball paint chart, it has to go.

Poeticks: Ethereal? Really? Words like 'gossamer' in poetry work like a bright red sports car for a driver who wants to impress: they promise more than they deliver. The English language is one of the richest in the world and all of its words are at your disposal but use them judiciously. Sometimes 'shard' will be the right word, but nine times out of ten it sounds self-conscious and frilly. Don't confuse a love of language with the use of long words. The resonance of a successful poem usually lies not in linguistic somersaults, but in simple phrases that capture a large emotion.

Word inversion: or, why it ridiculous to put a verb at the end of a sentence is. Writing 'Upon her I did gaze', or 'down the street I walked' etc., is the way that Yoda would write, not a twenty-first century poet. Yes, Keats *did* do it and in his time it was wonderful. Why, I am sometimes asked, don't current poets use these old tropes? For the same reason that you don't wear a crinoline to work. It's a free country and you can do it if you like, but you'll look daft. We need to understand our own cultural environment, not as slavish followers but as artists who appreciate the context in which we make art. As ever, reading contemporary poetry gives you a feel for that context.

Mind the gap: line breaks. White space on the page is not arbitrary. It's a subtle part of the craft and I'm not convinced that one can teach it. At least, I'm not convinced that I can teach it. The best way to learn it is (you guessed it) by looking at the poems you love, to see what function the line breaks serve. Read Sharon Olds, Philip Larkin and EE Cummings for three different approaches to line breaks. Remember that line breaks are flexible, and don't have to fall where the gaps in speech fall. Break a line mid-sentence to make a strong rhyme operate more subtly or use a break as a spotlight, to visually highlight something on the page. Here's a simple example. In Charles Bukowski's poem *Barfly* he says:

> ...but give me one truly alive woman
> tonight
> walking across the floor toward me

He could have written

> but give me one truly alive woman tonight,
> walking across the floor toward me

Instead he sets the word 'tonight' on a line of its own. It gives a sense of immediacy and urgency, highlighting the need and incidentally giving us a simple, hungry image.

Line breaks can create a little cliff-hanger, making you anticipate the next word. They can emphasise the last word in a stanza or create a feeling of space and air, slowing down the action. The break is a unit of structure, grouping parts of a poem together almost like chapters of a novel. It can disrupt sense, giving a feel of incoherence if your narrator is traumatised or confused.

Play around with breaks as you work on the poem, to see what effect they have on pace or tone. Whatever you do with them, do it for a reason. A few years ago there was a sudden outbreak of couplets in journals and competitions, because it so happened that three shortlistees in the National Poetry Competition had written in couplets (verses of two lines). They weren't successful because they wrote in couplets. They each wrote a good poem, which needed to be in couplets for some of the reasons above.

Gerunds: Frisk your poem for an excess of 'ings'. 'He was wearing' could be 'he wore'; 'the wind was blowing' could be 'the wind blew'. Patterns of repetition and sound are part of the poem's engineering, and must be engineered. Too many 'ings' look messy and scatter syllables all over the place. That attention to detail is what makes the best poems sound effortless and natural. If this seems pernickety, you may have chosen the wrong art form.

Rhyme: On a spectrum of rhyme where one end reads CAT/ SAT/ MAT and the other end reads ORANGE/ SNOOKER TABLE, the possibilities are limitless. The best way to learn what rhyme can do is – you guessed it – to seek out the best current and past poetry. Take time to savour the chimes in sound that may not be immediately clear – see my chapter on reading for some pointers. Rhyme need not be a crude tool, always falling at the end of a line and precisely echoing its pair word. Half rhymes like *peer / pore,* or echoing sounds like *half / have* give a poem structure without drawing the reader's attention to the scaffolding that holds it up. Read Philip Larkin for subtle and solid rhymes, or Wendy Cope for rhyme in the service of wit.

Poets writing for performance may get particular value from rhyme, which signposts an audience through the piece, but too much rhyme is boring. Repetition, simple refrains or internal rhymes also hold the hearer's attention without being predictable. A strong rhyme, suddenly broken with a non-rhyming line, can shock us out of complacent listening. Shake it up. Whatever your style, make a point of reading or watching poets who don't write in your idiom, and find their strong points. Falling into a rut is not good for your creative muscles. Get onto YouTube and the Poetry Foundation app to sample a wide range of styles. Hollie McNish, Mark Grist, Michael Rosen and Patience Agbabi will give you a good sample to begin with.

Stress-test metaphors or similes: especially the ones that you are most proud of. The opposite of cliché is surprise. Original, surprising language makes us look at something anew but if it's there *only* to surprise, it can feel gimmicky. Your metaphor has to work at both ends. When Homer tells us about the 'wine-dark sea' that works because the sea is dark and so is wine. By all means be fanciful, but let your fanciful phrases evoke the image you want.

Be true, not accurate. Most poetry is broadly autobiographical. It may be very important to you to tell the whole truth – but you are writing a poem, not a witness statement. Give yourself permission to stray from precise facts if it helps the work. Change a detail if it makes your story clearer. It can be a positive liberation to flip the gender, colour or relationships of people in the poem. The dog may have been called Rover in real life, but a dog called Tyson or Fifi will quickly signal something about the owner. Your narrator could be female instead of male… and so on.

A poem is a compressed piece of writing, and we zip a lot of meaning into a few lines so a slight tweak may help with clarity. If, for instance, you report a conversation between two women, you need to be very clear which 'she' or 'her' is meant in every line. If one of them becomes a man, that little hurdle is removed because one party is now a 'he' and it will be much clearer who is speaking. You can also improve the sound qualities of the poem without compromising your integrity. For instance, if you describe someone eating an apple – does it have to be an apple? Does 'pear' or 'plum' offer a better rhyme or sound? Be true, not accurate. As Glyn Maxwell says in *On Poetry*:

> Make the poem bright at the reading, true in the echo, strong to the ear, right by the eye.

CHAPTER ELEVEN
Why Use Poetic Form?
by Mona Arshi

'Form is a body. Verse form literally embodies the emotion of the poem. In the sense that embodiment both is and contains the life it is the body of.' – Molly Peacock [1]

I need to talk to you about form. The word 'form' itself is a peculiar, loaded, aloof abstract, and a singularly unhelpful term. The fact that academics and critics have pored over, examined and attempted to reach for answers as to why form matters to poems should tell you something about the challenges that the idea of form brings.

Part of the problem with this concept in the context of poetry is that some poets have come to understand the concept of form through their association with traditional poetic verse forms. Given the fact that 90 percent of contemporary poetry is written in free-verse, some poets believe that form is not important or that it is an irrelevant archaic relic of the past. I would like to tell you that form, the idea of form, is about more than being skilled at crafting villanelles, the sonnet forms or getting to grips with chain-rhyme terza rimas. Though of course, these are a part of the story of form. Having said that, if you haven't read forms closely or attempted to write in traditional verse forms because you think they are restrictive and you want to express yourself in a freer way, I would ask that you reconsider and challenge your prejudices.

All poetic forms fascinate me. I find Western traditional forms appealing and use them as equally as I read and use non-Western forms, such as the ghazal form, the renga, the tanka, and the landay. I am equally enriched by prose poems written

---

1   Quoted in, *On Form Poetry, Aestheticism, and the Legacy of a Word,* Angela Leighton (OUP, 2007).

by James Tate and Charles Simic as those that walk and talk the prose poem but may not be one, such as poetic utterances by Lydia Davies. I love the ballad form because the form is to be used for something specific; telling us a story (usually a pretty grisly one) before printing presses were around, written in a bumpy meter which turned on your ear so you could keep it in your memory and pass it on. In 2014, I wrote a poem about the horror of an honour killing in ballad form. Equally, I write in ghazals because the trembling long lines can somehow bear holding the lyric music, and the refrain's echoes at the back of this music are like an ache, like heartache.

Some poets believe (wrongly, in my opinion) that writing in traditional form stifles the imagination; I think it's liberating. Sometimes a sort of elation occurs when a form's purpose is fulfilled and the poem has somehow found its own rightness.

Form is your friend. Forms are for something. Yes. Even if you only choose to write in free verse. I mainly write free verse too, but I also know that I can reach for more traditional forms should the poem demand it. Should the poem demand it. You may have a particular view of what the poem should be but the poem in front of you may have different ideas. Every poem has its own form. Do remember that you are making something, after all. You have to be equally attentive to the form of what you are writing into; form includes (but is not limited to) considerations such as shape and length and verses. You could walk into your house having captured this poem – this incredible creature, this slippery yellow-veined translucent thing – and you may have the best syntax and most arresting images, but if you haven't paid attention to form you are letting down your precious, hard-won, captured poem. As poets, just as you are writing into the poem and discovering the poem, you are simultaneously discovering the form. Form does not exist purely as some sort of vessel or vase that you pour the poem into, and I don't think that this inside/outside image is particularly helpful. Form makes you see the world of your poem in language more clearly. Conversely, if your form is getting in the way of your poem, maybe you should reconsider your form? Form should not be an afterthought. Also, form shouldn't cough, or if it coughs, you definitely shouldn't be able to hear it.

As with all things associated with poetry, reading other poets, the masters of form, will help an awful lot. Or better still, get taught by an amazing tutor. Most of what I know about poetry is due to my mentor, the poet Mimi Khalvati.

Experiment with different forms; shorter, more condensed forms, for example. Look back at your poetry, or ask another poet friend nicely to do this. Are you reverting to a particular default form? Sometimes what's helpful is to shut down the strongest sense; close your eyes and try and listen to the poem in your head after you've captured it. Often our initial instincts about a poem are very good ones.

Remember that life is too short to be writing in one form, even if you are really adept at that form. Nowadays, after I finish a poem, I try to defend its form in my head. Why the lengths? Why the shorter end lines, why the prosaic form? Why oh why have I reached for couplets again? Try to begin a conversation with form if you haven't already done so, and always remember that you are making something.

Mona Arshi was born in West London where she still lives. She worked as a Human Rights lawyer for a decade before she received a Masters in Creative Writing from the University of East Anglia. Her debut collection, *Small Hands,* published by Pavilion Poetry, part of Liverpool University Press, won the Forward Prize for best first collection in 2015.

CHAPTER TWELVE
On the Third, Seventh and Fifty-Third Draft: Fine Polishing

'I write one page of masterpiece to ninety-one pages of shit. I try to put the shit in the wastebasket.' – Ernest Hemingway

It's comforting to know that Hemingway felt like that too. But it doesn't help with working out which of the ninety-two pages on your desk/ floor/ recycling bin is the one worth saving.

For me, the finished poem is usually no more than five or six drafts after the first one. Don Paterson, by contrast, once said that he can make seventy or eighty drafts of a poem. Whatever your preference, the last stage of editing is a vital part of making the work work. Admit where you are being self-indulgent or mawkish. Examine the poem to make sure it is more than a snapshot of your holiday, or a private exchange (it may start as either one, but your declaration of love for your daughter has to move *me* too and I've never met her). Above all, ask yourself: is this poem *boring*? Does it offer the reader anything?

Be bold in your edits. It's poetry, not open heart surgery. Often we are too timid, as if a poem was delivered by some mystical stroke of luck and will be spoiled by too much intervention. You wrote it, and you can work on it without destroying it. Sometimes you need to turn a poem upside down or inside out, and take a great part of its substance away to make the essential parts shine. Anything you do can be reversed, especially if working on the computer.

What does that mean in practice? I'll illustrate with two versions of my poem *Mallaig.* Exhibit A is not the very first draft, which went into the recycling bin long ago. That would have been a page of notes with no form, just ideas and phrases. The draft shown here is probably the second one, where I sift out all the phrases and ideas that seem worth exploring and type them into the computer.

Read it, write all over it, scribble your queries or criticisms. Get your revenge on the bossy *How to Be a Poet* woman. Think about what's wrong with it. Whatever effect it has on you, try and home in on the *words* creating that effect. That's what to do with each draft of your own work; focus right in on the parts that work and the parts that don't work. If this looks nothing like your own early drafts, don't panic. You are not doing it wrong – just differently to me.

Mallaig (Draft)   Jo Bell

Where are they at this moment
all the seals and whales,
the fat slick creatures of the sea?
Their world is larger than ours.
Their landmarks smell of fish.

Early in a morning slant with rain,
I stepped out for a first fag
on the wind-whipped harbour wall
and understood that there,
beyond the sleeping ferry boats and ketches
was a whale.
There was a tension
in the tons of brine, a shift of waters,
wait: a great slow
sigh of breath.

The muscled blowhole closed.
The deep blank beast turned back to sea,
back to the known – to comforts
of buoyancy and kelp.

Somewhere in that drenching world
are whales and seals
with leather-bottle bodies
who measure time as *now* or not at all,
who graze the mile-deep plains
who loom like salty stoics
and make their brisk and mottled journeys
on the broad ways between isles.
For us, only the islands meaning much;
for them, only the spaces between.

The waves throw up their flints and handkerchiefs
against the dark wet walls, the women,
the curious beasts at the edge of the world.

The woman was me. I was indeed at the little port of Mallaig on the west coast of Scotland. I had stayed overnight in a local B&B, and was going to catch a ferry to Skye later. I'm not sure if I actually saw a whale in the harbour, but I thought I did.

Even in this early draft, I had already made some decisions. I didn't want it to be just a 'here is what happened to me on my holiday' poem, which is very common and holds little interest for the reader. I wasn't sure what the poem was about, but it wasn't about me. So, I decided to put it in the third person; it's not 'I' but 'a woman' who stands at the harbour wall. She needs a reason to pause at the harbour – something to suggest an ordinary private moment, not a romantic stroll or a working day. So she is lighting up a fag. I said that she had 'stepped out' to give the sense of a fleeting moment. I meant to show that her home was nearby and she'd be back there in a few minutes. I didn't know why that was important, I just did it and liked it.

That small decision illustrates how a poem can pivot on one choice. Did I choose those words 'stepped out' to highlight the contrast between the woman, rooted in one spot, and the whale, untethered? Or did an arbitrary choice of words suggest that contrast and led me to think about it further? I'm not sure, but if I had written 'stops the car' instead of 'steps out' it would offer other possibilities. That would have suggested a woman who herself is in motion, like the sea creatures, and the poem might have gone in a different direction. It's at this molecular level that a poem begins to accrete and take shape. Pay attention to every choice of word, and see where it might lead.

The draft is already called 'Mallaig'. I wanted a sense of place, even if my reader doesn't know where that place is. Place names always retain some flavour of the culture they spring from. Yet I left out the details of what the houses look like, what the local shops or streets are called, because it isn't a portrait of the town: it's about a woman and a whale. I wanted to sketch a simple place on the edge of things, where a whale and a woman might meet, so I used simple physical props –

rain, the quay, a ferry. I used the word 'ketch' rather than just 'boat' because even if you don't know what a ketch is, it is the proper word and lends authenticity. I wanted to suggest heavy rain without saying 'it was raining heavily' – hence the idea of a 'morning slant with rain'. It's a bit odd, because it was a bit odd.

There are some ideas here that I liked, and one or two which I liked so much that they had to go. I was thoroughly pleased with my 'leather bottle seals'. I asked if this was an indulgence, but decided that it was a good physical image and a reader would get the idea. My 'salty stoics', however, fell by the wayside. I have a keen interest in Stoic philosophy, but you might not. It's an abstract idea, when I like to stick with the physical where I can, and I feared it was pretentious. When I've shown the draft to people subsequently, they are all very keen that the salty Stoics should remain, so perhaps this was the wrong decision.

I felt that the end was too trite and cod-philosophical. It took the slight weirdness of the moment and made it into a full-blown Gothic, so it had to go. The beginning, with its questions, felt like an important bit of content but I suspected these words were in the wrong place. The reader was thrown into the questions without understanding who was asking them or what the circumstances were.

The draft is baggy and unstructured, as it might well be at this stage. A draft exists as the first stage of something else, with no more resemblance to the finished object than a length of cloth has to the three-piece suit it becomes. We have to be relaxed about that, and work out as we go along what structure the content lends itself to. Finally, though it expresses ideas which occurred to me as I stood there, I didn't write 'It occurred to me as I stood there...'. Obviously it occurred to me. It's my poem.

There were probably four or five revisions between the draft above and the published version, overleaf:

66

Mallaig (published version)   Jo Bell

One early morning slant with rain
a woman steps out for a first smoke on the quay
and understands that there,

between the greyscale ketch and ferry,
is a whale. There's tension in the tons of brine,
a shift of waters, wait –

an epic sigh. The blowhole clenches
and the deep blank beast turns back to sea,
toward the known; its buoyant safeties, pod and kelp.

In that drenched world are sparks of fish
and leather-bottle seals: a populace
who measure time as *now* or not at all

who graze the mile-deep plains,
make brisk and mottled journeys
on the thousand ways between our isles.

Where are they now – wet brethren,
fat slick creatures of the sea?
Their landmarks smell of fish.

They move through larger worlds
with no idea of weather,
cigarettes, necessity.

Poetry is writing with pattern. If it has no pattern at all – neither of sound, of rhythm, of rhyme, of visual shape or repetition – then it may not be a poem at all. As I wrote, this one seemed to suit tercets (three line stanzas). They weren't arbitrary. Each one had to make sense on its own as a unit, or lead into the next one. I used line breaks to slow it down and build suspense, especially with that instruction 'wait - ' which makes you do just that. I moved the questions to the end of the poem, shifted the scene-setting lines to the start and removed the portentous and clunky ending of the draft. I wanted to leave the reader with a lingering sense of two worlds with different priorities; so I came back at the end to the cigarette which was lit at the beginning.

Perhaps I did it all wrong. In that case, you can decide exactly what I did wrong and how you would handle it differently. At any rate, consider these common mistakes that can make the difference between an arresting poem and a so-so one.

Sequence: Let's say that after a good deal of work, you have a poem of four stanzas. It has taken you a lot of time and effort to get here, and you are rather pleased with yourself. However, something is wrong. Could it be the order of the stanzas? Look at the whole poem as objectively as you can. What is the most striking or interesting line, and could it sit right at the beginning? Could your stanzas 1,2, 3 and 4 be rearranged with a bit of work – 4, 2, 3, 1 for instance? The most interesting part may be buried in the middle of the piece. Disrupt order. Tell the story backwards, or start in the middle. Most important, don't be afraid to cut out acres of text where you have got bogged down in explanation or detail.

First line: Look at the first-line index of a good poetry anthology. Which poems do you immediately want to read? Which ones do you gloss over? The single most common failure of poems is that they start where the actual events started, and not where the poem should start. Novelists share this difficulty. A novelist friend admitted to his editor that his first couple of chapters were admittedly a bit dull, but the reader wouldn't understand the main story (which really kicked off in chapter three) without them. The editor brutally pointed out that the reader would never get to chapter three, because she would have already put the book aside.

Readers can enjoy a 'slow burner' that gradually reveals itself, but there is a difference between an unfolding poem and one that is merely dull at the beginning. By the time you've finished your drafts, the beginning of the poem is no longer the place where the writer got in and began to feel their way around. It's how the Unknown Reader gets in, and begins to see what the writer had to say. Sadly, the Unknown Reader owes you nothing. The Unknown Reader has other poems available to them. They come across yours in an anthology, a magazine, a website – and if it bores them they will simply move on to the next one, as you would yourself. They are busy. They are late for the train. So get right in at the beginning, with a line which makes the reader want to follow your thread to the end. Make them miss the train.

Last line: The end of your poem is where you leave the reader. S/he goes off to wash the dishes or conduct brain surgery, still thinking about what you wrote. The last line is like the sounding of a gong, which will reverberate in the reader's mind as they continue their day. A quiet, slow-burning phrase will keep working over the next hours and days, giving to the person who read it access, not only to *your* great wisdom, but to their own.

The temptation for the poet is always to continue a little longer than they should. I often wound writers' feelings by asking, 'Could you lose the last two lines?' After all, if you've done that work of 'show, don't tell' in the piece, then you don't need to reiterate at the end. Read the poems you love and really scrutinise the endings. Look at the end of *Ozymandias*.

Shelley shows us the words on a fallen monument:

> 'My name is Ozymandias, king of kings:
> Look on my works, ye Mighty, and despair!'
> Nothing beside remains. Round the decay
> Of that colossal wreck, boundless and bare
> The lone and level sands stretch far away.

He doesn't add as many poets would, 'And I thought to myself, how ironic that such a statue should survive, when the culture that made it has failed.' He has *shown* us that with visual images. The last line is a picture of barrenness. The reader leaves the poem with a sense of emptiness and loss. Trust your own imagery and the mood you've created. Don't over-egg it with a neat explication. The reader is not dim; the reader is you.

Title: A reader once told me that he felt the title of a poem worked with the last line, to act like the two ends of a swimming pool. 'You reach the end of the pool, and the ripples bounce right back to the other end: you reach the last line of the poem, and the ideas reverberate back to the title.' And so they do. The title of your poem is not just the name that you give it to help with filing, so that you can find it again. It is a vital part of the architecture. The title may seem obscure at first but seen again, after the end of the poem, it may prove the key to understanding. Alternatively there's the title which seems childishly simple, but gains in meaning as the poem unfolds. It's a signpost to what the poet considers significant. John Lindley's poem 'Missing Children', about children he never had, is deliberately ambiguous – is he missing them, or are they simply missing?

The title can lift a lot of weight from the body of the poem, freeing you to start with a strong or surprising line. The reason that poems are often dull at the start is that's where we put all the scene-setting. You don't *really* want to spend the first four lines explaining that the poem takes place as you're packing a bag to leave home, but how else can you make that clear? Call it 'Packing to Leave Home' and deliver the reader straight into the story.

The title is a good place to park ambiguity or suggest a longer back-story, without making the poem clunky. Call it 'What She Said Next' and we understand that an important episode has already happened off screen, as it were. You may be writing about what your dad said to you at the petrol station but if you call it 'Last Words', or 'The Day I Came Out', or 'Meanwhile My Mother Was Leaving', the conversation takes on a different dimension. Billy Collins' wonderful poem about the neighbour's dog barking incessantly as Collins tries to listen to Beethoven is called 'Another Reason Why I Don't Keep A Gun In The House'. If you call a poem 'Autumn' and then begin 'It is autumn' or 'the leaves are falling again' that's a missed opportunity to make the title really work.

Listen: As counselled by Jonathan Davidson in Chapter Four, read your work *aloud*. Seriously. If you hear errors, sticking points or places where the rhythm doesn't work then change them. This can be an astonishing transformer of your writing. If you have the stomach for it, read the poem to someone else without priming them as to what the poem is about, or what you want them to notice. Ask them afterwards what they remember. It will almost always be a concrete image; not the abstract ideas, but the physical language of touch or smell. This has been my single biggest lesson in poetry, and I have learned it over and over again. For me, the five senses are where we have to root every poem. For you, this exercise may be more a question of balancing rhyme or punctuation, or keeping the pace of a narrative. If you can't read your poem without fainting for lack of breath, you need more commas.

That thing you always do: As you accumulate more poems, look for patterns in your work. Ask every now and then if you're falling into a rut. Challenge yourself to start in a more direct way, or cut out the stylistic tics that you lean on. Are your poems always roughly the same length? If sending a poem to a competition, is it always just skimming the maximum length allowed? Try whittling your piece down to a four- or eight-liner and see if it is improved. Do you always use rhyme, or never use rhyme? Are you telling yourself that you love free verse when actually you're too idle to write in form – or telling yourself that you love traditional forms because you don't have the confidence to try free verse? Try whatever technique might better suit the content of the poem. Surprise yourself.

That thing everyone else always does: As you write and rewrite, keep in mind Glyn Maxwell's scathing characterisation of the universal contemporary poem:

> I look at something, but obviously it reminds me of something else. Which I saw once, somewhere way more interesting than my room is. So I carry on like this, until I guess I've created a sort of mood. Then I'm just about ready to end on some striking point that makes you think a bit. (from *On Poetry*)

He's being mean, of course. A lot of very good poems follow roughly this pattern. But we may as well admit that there *are* predictable and commonplace formats, and commonplace subjects too. You know this because of course you read contemporary poetry all the time in journals, books, and at live readings. The poem by someone who has discovered a photograph, showing her parents years before she was born, has been written many times. The poem that tells us of the writer's childhood in rural Wales or suburban Idaho, the experience of giving birth or the strange feeling of historical connection when visiting the Pyramids, likewise.

There's no need to avoid any of these subjects, which are valid and moving in the right hands. Revisit old subjects by all means. You might as well, because there are no new ones. Just do it carefully enough to hold a jaded reader's attention, and with an awareness of the great poems already in circulation. Your life is your own. Your experience is different to that of any other person, which is why you want to write it. But your life is also similar in some respects to *the readers'* lives – which is why we want to read it.

Mind your language: The Unknown Reader is not an idiot who needs an explanation of every reference – but neither is s/he psychic. If you speak Gujarati at home or you use a particular jargon in your job, certain words may seem self-explanatory to you. This private knowledge can enrich your poetry, but try it out on someone who doesn't know the idiom. One person was astonished that nobody in our writing group knew what a *neonate* was, a phrase she used surprisingly often. (It means 'newborn', a word which worked just as well in the final poem. She was a midwife.) If your style is dense, richly textual, layered, experimental or metaphysical, fill your boots; but a poem is not a crossword puzzle to be solved. We can't excuse wilful obscurity by saying that the reader has to pull her weight. You have to pull yours too.

Process: It's hard work, editing. It's not like working in a coal mine but it makes demands on you all the same. When you get stuck or tetchy, interrupt yourself. Anthony Trollope, whose *Autobiography* is full of writerly insights, did three hours of writing every day and then stopped. Go for a walk. Knit something. Watch the Grand Prix. Read *Lives of the Caesars*. Any one of these may feed into the poem.

When you think it is finished, put it out of sight for a week, a year, a decade. Personally, I find that more than a month does no good, but many people find a longer break helpful. When you return to the poem, you look at it with refreshed eyes and a little more objectivity. At this stage, be stern with yourself. Is it boring? Is anything on the page there solely to show off?

Tense: In the process of writing and revising, you may try out different tenses or simply use different tenses by accident. In the first stanza, your narrator 'looked out of the window' in the past tense, but in the third stanza he 'picks up the phone' in the present tense? This is a really common thing to overlook. At best, it looks sloppy; at worst it makes the sense of the poem hard to grasp.

Sweat the small stuff: Grammar matters. There are particular registers of language – when writing in dialect, or as a child for instance – which need to be imprecise because that's how we speak in daily life. But simple grammatical errors will usually make you look ignorant. Here's a very common one, especially for those of us who are northern English: you can say 'he stood' or 'he was standing', but not 'he was stood'. If you aren't deliberately writing dialect, then it's just bad English. Likewise, 'she sat' or 'she was sitting' – never 'she was sat'. Poetry is about the careful deployment of every word. If every syllable matters, then we need to pay attention to them all.

There are other tics or habits which clutter up a line in poetry, though they wouldn't matter in prose. Here's an example. The past pluperfect is the tense used to incorporate two levels of past activity. If someone writes, 'We moved to Nottingham in 1975 because my father *had grown up there*,' we know that both the moving and the growing up are in the past, but that the growing up was farther back in time. It's very useful in the right place. Used too often, the pluperfect scatters the word 'had' over a page like confetti. Look at this extract from a *Guardian* article by Martin Sixsmith (January 21st 2017), which is perfectly fine as a news story:

> One woman from Yorkshire… told me of her brother's arranged marriage with a relative from Pakistan. The relationship **had** gone wrong and their father **had** taken the girl back to her native village and dumped her there. Her family **had** been dishonoured, so when the father next came to Pakistan the girl's cousin **had** murdered him.

In a news article the writer's purpose is to get the information across. The reader won't even notice the tense here. In a poem, however, sounds matter. The pluperfect can create graceless extra syllables which make for a clunky rhythm. The reader might not know why, but the writer should. If he were frisking his paragraph for contraband syllables, Sixsmith might write, 'The relationship went wrong and their father took the girl back to her native village…. Her family was dishonoured, so when the father next came to Pakistan the girl's cousin murdered him.' Can you change the tense in your poem to streamline it? This level of scrutiny is what makes the good stuff stand out, on the page and in the ear.

The heavy artillery: big solutions. After all that editing, sometimes a poem just doesn't work. It doesn't say what you wanted to. It sounds trite or pompous or whiney. You have tried everything you know but you simply can't fix it. In these cases, there are two remedies.

The first is last-ditch surgery. Consider these techniques:

- Turn it upside down – re-order the stanzas and see if you get a punchier piece.
- Cut it down to three lines. What's essential?
- Can the title help to expand or clarify?
- Write it from a different point of view.

The second option, when you've tweaked it for weeks or months and it still doesn't work – is to give up on it. Honestly. I speak as someone who once took twelve years trying to nail a particular poem (I broke for meals). Finally it did fall into place, but sometimes it just won't. When you absolutely cannot make it better, give it one more draft. Then throw it away. It may be that the point of this poem was simply to teach you how to write the next one. So long as you learned something along the way, it was not a wasted effort. As the author John C. Maxwell has it, 'sometimes you win – sometimes you learn'. How did you learn to read, or ride a bike, or drive? How did you learn about relationships or cooking? By getting it wrong until you got it right. You don't consider the third driving lesson a failure because you only got your licence after the twentieth. You don't consider early training sessions wasted, because only this year did you run a marathon. Writing is no different in that we learn as we go along, but with poetry you never arrive at the finish line. You become more skilled, but never quite able to express – or indeed to identify – everything you want to say. After all, the very things we want to say evolve from year to year. You can't always keep up with yourself. By developing a writerly toolkit, however, you will be *almost* ready to express what you need to, at this moment in your life; and better equipped to meet the next one.

✍ Top Tips

Think about how to keep track of drafts as you work on a poem. Sometimes as you look at the overwrought wordplay of Draft 23, you yearn for the spontaneity of Draft 1, or vice-versa. If you're working on a computer, you may be over-writing your earlier poem every time you work on it. Consider starting each revision by copy-and-pasting the last version, then working on the copy, so that you have a thread of revisions. Clear out the files every six months, to discard long-dead drafts. Now, to business.

CHAPTER THIRTEEN
Making Peace with Poetry
by Robert Peake

Introduction

'I was diagnosed as a poet here several years ago,' she quipped. I was exploring graduate programmes in creative writing, speaking to an administrator by phone. I knew she was being cheeky, and that this was just one of her catchphrases. Still, the idea of relating to poetry like a chronic illness struck me as partly absurd, but partly fitting.

At this point in my life, I was on a quest to discover what it means to be a poet, and most importantly, what it means to me. More than being stuck with a lifelong condition, what I really wanted to know was how to stick with poetry over time, having seen many other talented writers fall away from it, and having fallen away from it once myself.

In my early twenties, I abandoned poetry in an effort to 'put away childish things'. It only seemed appropriate in anticipation of becoming a parent. Yet it was soon after I became a father that the necessity of poetry came back to me – in the neonatal intensive care unit of our local hospital, holding my infant son in my arms for the very last time.

I was cast into a period of agonised questioning – of my ambitions, my identity, and the nature of life itself. In poetry, I rediscovered a means to engage the complexity of human experience on its own terms – not as a reductive catchphrase, marketing slogan or political sound bite – but as an expansive and containing act of art. Poetry was big enough to hold me in its arms as I raged through that dark time.

I wanted more. Michael Langley famously said that, 'If I knew where poems came from, I'd go there.' I wanted to know, and I wanted to go there. What's more, I was willing, as William Stafford demanded, to revise not only my work, but my life.

I knew that being a poet had something to do with longevity, and suspected that the elder poets who had managed to sustain a life steeped in poetry knew something – something that I was desperate to find out. I could see it in the twinkle in their eye. Charles Bukowski said, 'Show me an old poet and I'll show you, more often than not, either a madman or a master.' I was ready to find out which was which, and to become either, if it meant a lifetime taking part in this great conversation, this containing embrace.

What follows is what I found out along the way. I feel strongly that to become a poet is more something one catches than learns by rote. Perhaps in this way it is not so much a chronic illness as a kind of virus to which one must stay constantly exposed. That's a bit gross. So, I prefer instead to think of it as a love affair that requires continuous re-kindling. My real quest, then, has been to stay in love with poetry, come what may.

This quest unfolded in three stages – first, the quest to make peace with the world, then the quest to make peace with myself as a poet, and finally the quest to make peace with the mysterious nature of poetry itself.

I. Making peace with the world

'On the one hand, it's <u>poetry</u>; on the other hand, it's just poetry.'
– Marvin Bell

Writing this at the beginning of a Trump presidency in the US, with the consequences of the Brexit vote looming here in the UK, it has never been more clear to me that the world both desperately needs the humanising effect poetry can have, and that it also quite simply doesn't 'get it'.

Looking at it a certain way, there would seem to be a lot at stake for poets as well. Like many in the arts, poets are willing to persevere in the face of a tidal wave of rejection. If they were salesmen, their goods would be one of two types: very expensive, or very cheap.

That is, they might be like the luxury yacht salesman who only needs one or two sales per year to bring in a big commission cheque, and so is willing to put up with a lot of 'no's to get there. This would imply that poetry is incredibly valuable.

But wait you say – they might simply be desperate, like the roadside flower salesman, putting up with the 'no's not from luxury, but necessity – implying that what they are peddling is actually quite cheap.

So, which is it? Is poetry essentially invaluable, or is it nearly worthless?

This sense of duality has been the impetus for journalists in our time, citing select statistics, to frequently declare poetry so worthless as to actually be 'dead', and for poets to retort with impassioned anecdotes illustrating that its vitality and necessity has never been greater. Could it be that poetry is in fact both (statistically) dead and (anecdotally) living? This makes poetry sound like some kind of quantum physics experiment, or even a zombie.

A less grisly and far more satisfying answer came to me in the form of a cult-classic book called *The Gift* by Lewis Hyde. In it, Hyde traces all manner of giving as it appears in anthropological studies and folk tales, and contrasts the cultural system of gift-giving with the familiar capitalist model of buying and selling.

This framework – of the marketplace on the one hand and the 'gift economy' (as he calls it) on the other – gave me a way to understand how poetry, through inhabiting both worlds, can be so rightly (and vehemently) regarded as both worthless and invaluable, depending on your perspective.

It is not only poetry, but the poet, who inhabits both worlds as well. So, I had to make peace with not one world but two. In my quest to learn how to navigate these two worlds effectively, I began teasing out and contrasting the qualities inherent in these two worlds:

Marketplace	Gift Economy
Transactions	Relationships
Quantity	Quality
Speed	Timelessness
Product	Process
Scarcity	Generosity
Fixed	Flow
Job	Vocation
Career	Way of life
History	The moment
Celebrity	Servant
Greatness (person)	Greatness (purpose)

According to the system of values on the left, dedicating one's life to poetry would seem utterly foolish. From the viewpoint on the right, however, there would hardly seem to be any more worthwhile course.

Yet the world we inhabit is overwhelmingly biased toward marketplace traits, and technology has generally only increased the rate at which these traits assert themselves and insert themselves into our lives. Social media, for example, is a poisoned well of jealousy – if you regard it that way – for any poet trying to 'make a career'. But in fact, the very idea that the arts should be a career in order to be legitimate is a marketplace notion as well.

Even for those who have seen beyond the marketplace qualities nearer the start of this list, and acknowledge that cultural importance must live side-by-side with marketplace values, the more insidious notions near the bottom of the list that one could 'make history' or achieve contemporary celebrity or enduring personal greatness all also belong to a more transactional, product-driven idea of art.

So, this world is constantly trying to pull us away from the very place where poetry gets made – in the moment and in the flow, in service to something greater than our (personal) selves.

The first peace I had to make, then, was to simply accept this duality. I inhabit it. Poetry inhabits it. When I look through one lens, I'm wasting my time as a poet; when I look through another, there's nothing I'd rather do.

I also had to acknowledge the necessity of both 'economies', both worlds – one to sustain life, the other to make life worth living.

Finally, I had to recognise the biases inherent in my conditioning as the product of a marketplace-focused society. We live in a strange post-fame era that is constantly trying to lure us into our fifteen minutes of Warhol-predicted fame. For me, it is not a few blips of viral web traffic that I'm after, but the means to sustain a love affair.

So, this foundation led me to my second quest: to make peace with myself as a poet.

II. Making peace with myself

'Poetry is just evidence of life. If your life is burning well, poetry is just the ash.' - Leonard Cohen

Recognising that poetry has its origins in the gift economy presents some unique challenges for poets living in a marketplace society. Robert Graves wryly observes that, 'There's no money in poetry, but there's no poetry in money, either'. Yet we all need to make a living. As much as each act of poetry is a gift to the self and to the world – as much as it is (as Mary Oliver points out) metaphorical bread for the metaphorical hungry, we still need actual bread when our bellies rumble.

Let me therefore refer to a brief tempering treatise on the perils of 'giving 'till it hurts' – a children's book called *The Giving Tree* by Shel Silverstein. While there is a certain poetry in the picture of the old man sitting on the stump-that-was-once-a-tree on the final page, the tree having given away in love to the man everything from fruit and branches to its very heartwood over time – I prefer to see it as a cautionary tale, and one particularly suited to poets.

It is important, for example, to charge market rates for market services – even if one doesn't make one's living as a poet. This is because others may be trying to make a living through poetry, and undercutting leads to a race to the bottom. Not everyone can pay with money, of course, and so it becomes ever more important to scrutinise one's motives (and bank balance) in deciding what poetry-related activities to pursue.

For me, working in an unrelated field in a flexible manner – such that I can rearrange my schedule for the odd reading – has given me a sense of freedom from needing poetry in a literal, survival-level sense. I have thus decoupled the desire to share my work from the desire to make ends meet, and this suits me. In fact, having a 'day job' has not sapped my creative verve, but actually redoubled my desire to succeed, on my own terms, at not only writing good poems, but at learning how to be a 'working poet'.

One day over breakfast, I found myself contemplating what 'success' might mean to me as a poet, and I scribbled this down on a napkin:

The secret to success is longevity
The secret to longevity is consistency
The secret to consistency is discipline
The secret to discipline is love

For some, the link between discipline and love may be the hardest to follow. Allow me to come back to that later, when we examine the nature of poetry. Suffice it to say that, in the end, success over the long term for me comes down to: staying alive, staying in the game, and staying in love with poetry.

Just as simple things like being honest about your feelings and taking out the recycling go a long way to making a romantic relationship work, so too did I find a few simple, practical techniques to keep the spark alive between poetry and me.

First, a brief word about self-image.

IIa. Warning: Don't try to be Baudelaire

Perhaps because the transaction-focused world doesn't understand poets, it throws up strange caricatures for us to emulate. The poète maudit, epitomised by everyone from Byron to Baudelaire, is a kind of tragic hero figure whose genius is only equalled by his ability to screw up his life.

It is a perverse and, in my view, inaccurate interpretation of the gift-versus-marketplace model to think that achieving some form of 'genius' in the arts gives one permission to make a mess of one's life (and the lives of those around them) – that is, that activity in one column alone could ever make up for, or cancel out, the other.

Yet he is a seductive devil, the maudit archetype, tempting us to burn bright and short when, in truth, we can bring far more light to the world and to ourselves through sustained luminescence. I have therefore chosen to take up as my motto the directive from Gustave Flaubert: 'Be steady and well-ordered in your life, so that you may be fierce and original in your work.'

This did not come easily. Temperamentally, I would say that I have a horror of routine. When my wife first met me, I was living more like Jack Kerouac – no schedule, no set routine, pulling 'all nighters' more as a matter of course than occasional necessity. I found out pretty quickly, however, that burning the candle at both ends soon leads to burning out. And you still have to clean up all that molten wax.

In the long run, real freedom for me came from giving measured attention to both worlds – marketplace and gift, responsibility and riotous creativity. I found that, when it comes to the practicalities of everyday living, the only way out is through.

In fact, this you-can-vindicate-your-screwy-lifestyle-through-art belief may not be the only unhelpful attitude you encounter as a poet who has been raised in a market-focused world. Like a child who has been raised by wolves, you may have a few things to unlearn (howling at the dinner table, perhaps?) to end up behaving most fully like the person you already are. I know I did. Some of them may be marketplace notions, others (like trying to emulate Kerouac) may be acts of rebellion against the marketplace that are equally unhelpful to sustaining a life steeped in creative encounter over the long term.

IIb. Exercise: Affirming (and re-affirming) what's true about poetry for you

To this end, I undertook a simple exercise to re-educate myself toward a more balanced point of view. You might want to try this yourself. On one side of a page, line by line and item by item, I wrote down all the unhelpful beliefs I had inherited from a world that likes to sneer at poetry. Then I shifted perspective to what I knew to be true about poetry. I got in touch with the essential poet within me, as best I could.

From this place, I wrote my own antidotes – line by line, rebutting each misbelief. Ideas like 'Poetry is a waste of time' became affirmations like, 'Poetry gives me the time and space to live a richer life'; 'There's not enough (prizes, publications, funding, etc.) to go around' became, 'When poetry wins, we all win'; 'Poetry is a childish fad' became, 'Poetry is part of who I am'. I ended up with about a dozen statements.

I tore off the column of unhelpful beliefs and binned them with gusto. Then I started reading back the list, affirming what I knew to be true. I liked the result of doing this so much, I made it a daily practice. These days, before I sit down to write, I read them all, twice – top-to-bottom and back again. In this way, I am not so much brainwashing myself as cleansing away the muck of market-focused misbelief, and preparing myself to write.

This simple practice has gone a long way toward keeping me in the game. But in itself, it didn't actually get the poems written. Robert Hass encouraged us to, 'Take the time to write. You can do your life's work in forty minutes per day.' This was the next peace I had to make – with myself in front of the blank page, and I had to make it over and over again.

IIc. Tip: Find your daily process

While reading my affirmations helped me get ready to write, never having to be 'at the beginning' helped even more. This is a trick I learned from my friend and mentor Marvin Bell: I keep a single document with all the false starts, half-baked ideas, snippets, phrases, and failed poems – everything I have written over the past decade. Each morning, I write down the date, and just start writing. Often, I'll scroll up and 'raid' previous material, bringing it down to work on it in another form. Here, my intention to be 'in the flow' matches the process of keeping one continuous document (which I back up regularly, of course).

In Leonard Cohen's terms, it is the ashtray into which I tip the 'ash' from a life that is 'burning well'.

Your approach may differ, but the key is this: a focus on process over product. As William Stafford said, 'A writer is not so much someone who has something to say as he is someone who has found a process that will bring about new things he would not have thought of if he had not started to say them.' So start. And start again. Daily, if you can. More importantly, find a way to keep starting and re-starting, no matter what.

IId. Tip: Find your tribe

I also had to make peace with myself as a poet among my contemporaries. It is in the middle of the choir that one learns best to sing. So too with reading and writing.

Part of my quest, then, was to find my 'tribe'– those poets with whom I could share, and from whom I could learn.

In pursuing these relationships – through books and through real human contact – continually bringing myself back to the right-hand column reasons for being in the game of poetry gave me the option to choose generosity over scarcity, quality over quantity, and the emotional content of the relationship over its material or transactional value.

In the end, if it comes down to making the right moves for my career or my soul, I know which will have the more enduring impact.

In seeking after this quality – of soul, of flow, of 'where poems came from' – I had to confront the third and most elusive quest–to make peace with the nature of poetry.

III. Making peace with the nature of poetry

'If I feel physically as if the top of my head were taken off, I know that is poetry.'– Emily Dickinson

Just as *The Gift* opened new understanding for me about how to reconcile the 'invaluable/worthless' duality in poetry, another cult classic, *Zen in the Art of Archery* by Eugen Herrigel, helped me to understand the mysterious nature of poetry itself.

In teaching and speaking, I sometimes get asked, 'What is poetry?' My simplest answer is that it is something we all know when we experience it, but that it is, by its very nature, hard to define.

In this way, my journey to be 'in the game' with poetry parallels Herrigel's study of archery with a Zen master in Japan. After years of practice and struggle within himself, one day the steps of the ritual practice all came together and in an effortless, graceful moment the arrow flew from his hand. The master bowed to him and said, 'It shot'

I read and re-read this passage, and realised that this, to me, described the essential nature of poetry. The reason I buy loads of books, go to readings in all manner of locations and venues, and write poetry myself – is to encounter that same kind of moment, that same presence. I call it, 'Poetry happened.'

It is that moment when the poet has succeeded, even briefly and partially, in using words to get beyond words. It is the moment in which the reader or listener has succeeded in following them. To say, 'Poetry happened' is not personal, and so not necessarily a compliment to the poet. It is more a simple observation or statement of truth. It is an experience I have been chasing all my life, and my heroes are those who make it (or perhaps let it) happen often.

Perhaps some of this experience is indeed physical, as Dickinson suggests – a unique combination of factors that spins our neurological tumblers into place, unlocking a burst of chemicals in the brain. I believe something more mysterious and wonderful may be happening as well, something that can only arise when one fully inhabits the present moment, as in Zen practice. A good poem, well received, resonates and transcends.

Yet as with the novitiate archer, most of the time it doesn't quite happen – or even happen at all! If the rejection rate in the marketplace is high, the failure rate in the context of the gift realm is equally formidable for poetry. How, then, to make peace with an art whose practice involves near-constant failure?

Here again, a focus on process over product goes a long way. Mihaly Csikszentmihalyi refers to a state called 'flow' – the relaxed, focused, and highly creative experience where one's skills are optimally matched to the challenge at hand. Elizabeth Gilbert talks about 'genius' not as an epithet, but a quality that visits the receptive. Czesław Miłosz has his 'daemon'; Federico Garcia-Lorca has his 'duende'. I love the idea of little goblins of inspiration flying over the rooftops, scanning for poets upon whom to descend. I also know that if I am not ready, they will pass me by.

So how to stay in this receptive state, this place of 'flow' where poetry can happen? Making peace with the nature of poetry for me has meant also making peace, in fact even embracing, my own failings in relationship to it. Marvin Bell liberatingly observed that, 'The good stuff and the bad stuff is all part of the stuff.' This has become a mantra when I sit down to write. In fact, the only criterion for success in my daily writing practice is that I keep doing it.

So, the focus is on letting poetry happen, the reality is that it rarely does, and the discipline is in persevering. This discipline is not self-punishment. It is like kindling one's passion for a distant lover who might one day return. It is a love for all who have gone before me and succeeded, and for all who persist in the face of a discouraging marketplace society to endeavour to make poetry happen. It is an honouring of myself and my poetic ancestors through the simple act of sitting down, and seeing what shows up.

The poet Sandford Lyne addresses the link between discipline and love in poetry beautifully in his poem 'Machado, Lorca, Neruda, Jiménez', concluding: 'You just want to be with them, / touch their sandals, wash their feet, / know a little of their courage, / walk, listen, learn: speak, / one day, perhaps, / one beautiful sentence / with those disciples of the word.'

This, more than anything, is what I wish for you dear reader: to know a little of the courage of our forebears in attempting to add your own beautiful sentence to the vast human scroll of poetry.

Conclusion

It was grief, love and courage that brought me back to poetry, and set me down once more upon the path. So, too, along the way I have had to grieve the nature of our market society, and my own misapprehensions about poetry. It has also been love that sustained me – or my forbears and teachers along the way, and the essence of poetry itself. No small amount of courage has been required as well, to take up the three-fold quest to make peace with the world, myself, and my chosen art.

As they say in the car adverts, 'Your mileage may vary.' In many ways, my own journey is just beginning. Of the great ceramicist Beatrice Wood, the critics observed that she did her best work in her nineties. (Which she attributed, by the way, to younger men and chocolate – so perhaps there's another tip for you.) Check back with me in another forty or fifty years and, while I may not have much new to say, my hope is that I will have deepened and sustained this practice. I might have even written a few more good poems along the way.

In the end, the biggest joke of all may well be that it was never about the poetry (as product) – but about the way that the practice of poetry shapes our lives. In the Zen practice of archery, there is a saying that, 'Whether or not you hit the target is none of your business.' Maybe Cohen had it right all along, that poetry is just some beautiful ash, that it was always about the way one's life was burning.

Here's hoping yours burns bright and long.

Robert Peake is an American-born poet living near London. He created the Transatlantic Poetry series, bringing poets together for live online readings and conversations. His film-poem collaborations have been widely screened in the US and Europe. He is a poetry surgery tutor for the Poetry Society in Hertfordshire, and writes for the *Huffington Post*. His next poetry collection *Cyclone* is forthcoming in July 2018 from Nine Arches Press.

CHAPTER FOURTEEN
Interrogating the Self
by Joelle Taylor

'Make it political as hell. Make it irrevocably beautiful.' – Toni Morrison

Poetry serves many purposes: poetry as beauty, as information, as anaesthetic, as pain, as journey, as political discovery. We are a broad church, and many of the congregation are atheists.

I want to feel changed when I read or listen to a piece, and so I expect the poet to have also experienced some internal shift, some change in their being, during the process of creating that piece. I self-define as a socio-political poet and so, understandably, I am more attracted to that writing and the nuance of the best work. Empathy is at the core of political writing, that ability or potential that an artist has to squeeze their bodies into the skin of another.

For my recent collection *Songs My Enemy Taught Me* (Out-Spoken Press, 2017) I not only conducted interviews and researched extensively, but also held a series of eighteen masterclasses across the UK with marginalised women from a variety of social and economic backgrounds – from rape survivors to refugees, girls affected by female genital mutilation to young Irish traveller women, from working class students to women in war zones. I used a technique that I'll call poetry reportage, a kind of investigative poetry, and close cousin to journalism. It is a poetic that attempts to be the carrier of a message, as much as it is about creating something aesthetically interesting.

The most difficult woman I had to interview for the book though was myself; after that, the rest seemed much easier and far friendlier. And they met my eye more often too. There is an argument that we always write about ourselves no matter our subject matter, and perhaps there is truth in that.

For the purposes of my book I treated myself like one of the marginalised women I worked with; I am indeed one of those marginalised women. I sat myself down, poured a thick coffee and asked myself the difficult questions. What is your name?

The first self-interview resulted in the title piece of the book, a seventeen-part canto that detailed my life journey from sexual abuse, though grief, loss of friendships and any sense of self, through mental illness and drug recklessness, and on toward ultimate survival, gentle rebellion, until finally arriving at the point I pick up a pen. In order to do that, I made a story board of myself.

To do this, write down no more than twelve scenes that reflect the passage of your life. Each scene must have a strong visual element, like a scene in a film. I sketch a lot while I am writing as that often throws forward the strongest metaphors. Time the process – only allow something like ten minutes for each visual scene before switching to another. Within the space of two hours you should have a clear idea of the moments in your life that are important to the core of you. Now: edit. You are looking for those scenes that are the most pivotal and powerful, as well as those with the strongest visual element. Why are these scenes the ones that seem the most important to you? Why is the overturned baby chair image that you can't stop thinking about a better description than a long narrative poem about domestic violence? Why is treating the bed sheet as a slowly developing photograph stronger than a descriptive passage about sexual abuse? I found a central metaphor based in fact that worked for me in writing the poem: my experience of abuse was at the hands of members of the military and so war became the central image, as well as the theme that linked the 60 odd other poems in the book.

The canto was the first poem that I have explicitly written with no intention of performing it. Whilst that has happened since publication, it was an important part of my development to forget the audience – just for once – to write something that imagines the audience as being alone. This poem is a secret. And it was an enormous relief and freedom to simply write something that will lie on the page, much as the 'I' in the poem once lay in bed as a child. I didn't have to try and fit word sequences into my wrong-shaped mouth, or place hidden rhymes that would help me memorise a piece.

Whilst writing these self-poems was a cathartic experience, that was not the reason for writing them; catharsis is a by-product of good poetry. If your poem only works for you, and is not aesthetically arresting, or beautiful or resplendent with extraordinary metaphors, then it's probably something you should keep for yourself. Don't forget to feed the messenger, the carrier of the message. This is especially important if you are writing for the page as your main audience. In the spoken word clubs I grew up in, it was necessary to write simple, didactic pieces with catchy messages and internal rhymes – because you only have 3 minutes to make yourself understood, often over bar-room clatter and to a distracted audience. The space created a poetry of insistence, of urgency. Writing for the page removes the need for that insistence. The reader has time to understand, to re-read and consider the depth of each image or metaphor. They have time to see themselves reflected in the surface of the page.

Writing the self is a powerful way to begin exploring poetry reportage; as poets we must make ourselves vulnerable in every way possible. It is through that door that change is waiting.

Joelle Taylor is an award-winning poet, playwright and author who has read her work nationally and internationally. She is the founder and artistic director of SLAMbassadors, the Poetry Society's pioneering national youth slam. She is a subject for study on the OCR GCSE curriculum and is a fellow of the RSA. She has released three collections of poetry, her most recent being *Songs My Enemy Taught Me* (Out-Spoken Press).

CHAPTER FIFTEEN
On Politics and Polemics

All ages are political, and this one more than most – including not just party politics but the power balances around gender, race, class, sexuality, disability and other topics that bring us into disagreement with each other. That brings us to polemical poetry. A polemic is a passionate argument, either in favour of something or against it. In practice it is usually 'against' because, by the time you are sufficiently moved to write about politics or social issues, you're already angry.

Poetry is a uniquely powerful outlet for such feelings. It can be anthemic, with refrains, rhymes or pointed repetition to rally an audience. It evolved specifically to make words memorable, and the most memorable protest poems outlive their own generation. Adrian Mitchell's famous 'To Whom It May Concern (Tell Me Lies About Vietnam)' remains relevant to any war. Linton Kwesi Johnson's 'Inglan is a Bitch' voices the experience of a Caribbean immigrant, Hollie McNish's 'Embarrassed' that of a young mother breastfeeding in a public toilet. Tony Walsh's 'This is the Place' had an immense healing impact in the aftermath of the Manchester bombing of 2017. Each is a rallying cry for those who share the poet's experience, and a window into such experience for those who don't.

Salena Godden, one of UK poetry's best performers, tells me that the spoken word scene has changed in the past year. In this time of seismic change across the UK, Europe and the US, she says, 'Audiences have doubled and there's a radical shift in the appetite for poetry.' Why? Because, she says, in times of great political or social change, poetry has three great weapons in its armoury. 'The poet can use fact, AND comedy, AND heart.'

Unfortunately the poet can also sound like a pub bore, preaching on Brexit or racism to a yawning audience who have heard it all before, and who probably come from the same demographic as the poet. Wislawa Szymborska complained that:

> young poets are often shocked that their poem about rebuilding post-war Warsaw or the tragedy of Vietnam might not be *good*. They're convinced that honourable intentions pre-empt form. But if you want to become a decent cobbler, it's not enough to enthuse over human feet. You have to know your leather, your tools, pick the right pattern, and so forth... It holds true for artistic creation too.

It is not enough to be angry. To get the message over, you need to be *good* and angry. It's easy to fall into 'virtue signalling' – although, to paraphrase author Joanne Harris, virtue signalling is better than signalling that you're an idiot. The poet has an opportunity to build solidarity, or inspire a change in behaviour. How, then, can you address the issues that matter most, and do it well?

Let's imagine that Poet X feels strongly about the microbeads used in cosmetics which are poisoning marine life. Here are a few tips that might help her:

Show don't tell. Cut out the abstracts – anger, frustration, heartbreak etc., – and use concrete images. Warsan Shire's pamphlet *Teaching My Mother How to Give Birth* covers war, female genital mutilation and the difficulty of growing up in two cultures. She does not explicitly say 'war is bad, FGM is an appalling practice' etc. Instead she *shows* us individuals, living real lives in which these things happen. Poet X could show us the physicality of ocean life, loading her poem with salty and muscular language so that we feel its value, rather than being *told* to feel its value.

Tell it from another point of view. Write something that happened to you as if it had happened to someone else, or from an opposing point of view. Poet X could write as an alien visitor wondering why we kill our sea creatures in this way, or as someone who simply does not care.

Start your poem in the middle. It can help to tell the story backwards, or in a random order. Leave some things out. Resist the temptation to deliver a sonorous moral at the end. Your choice of topic, title and content will have made your message very clear.

Wit is a weapon. Poetry on serious subjects doesn't have to be serious all the way through. Maya Angelou's poem 'Still I Rise' addresses deep racism and sexism, but maintains both humour and dignity. 'Does my sexiness upset you?/ Does it come as a surprise/ That I dance like I've got diamonds/ At the meeting of my thighs?' Salena Godden's best-known poem 'My Tits Are More Feminist Than Your Tits' is an escalating helter-skelter of ridiculous statements which mocks the way that women's bodies are discussed.

Praise is a weapon. Be positive about what you love, instead of negative about what you hate. If you loathe what is happening to the NHS, write in praise of nurses. If you are a petrolhead who resents speed limits, write about the joy of driving fast. If you feel single mothers get a bad deal, write a celebration of them. Poet X could call her poem IN PRAISE OF THE ANGLER FISH and start that way.

Be specific. Avoid mission creep, where your poem about Donald Trump's foreign policy becomes a list of *all* the things he's done wrong. Life is short, after all. Stick to one policy or statement. Instead of laying into a generic enemy like 'fat bankers' or 'the media', focus on one banker or headline. 'Politics is pointless without people,' says satirist Luke Wright, author of *Mondeo Man*. 'You apply it to people, and you can make a point.' For our Poet X, specificity may mean sticking to the issue of microbeads, rather than listing the many ways in which we pollute.

Do some research. Many of us write vague rants because we have only our opinion to work with. Read around the issue. Collect statistics. A shocking percentage or case study may give you a way into the poem.

Use different techniques and forms. Make a found poem out of headlines or bureaucratic forms. Quote a robotic telephone message or repeat a manifesto pledge over and over. Miss out whole phrases or lines, to mimic censorship. Use jargon or quotes. Poet X could list the ingredients in a body scrub, or the advertising slogan of a leading brand.

Performers: use your audience. Build in call-and-response lines, and encourage the audience to shout them with you. Exaggerate your characters to make them super-horrible. Luke Wright says that his Hogarthian characters 'remove it from reality slightly, so it becomes more powerful satire – making something that really exists extreme, exaggerating it to make it ridiculous'. Poet X might create an immensely vain character, washing his face with extract of dead dolphins in hopes of youth.

Ration your rhymes. On the page, perfect rhymes can sound comedic and overpower the poem. In performance, they are useful landmarks – but too much rhyme makes your work predictable. Surprise us with half-rhymes or a change of pace. There is no rule, by the way, which says that a poem for performance has to be three minutes long and performed at great speed. A short or slow poem can be surprising and effective.

Check your privilege. If you are a white person writing about black lives or a man writing about feminism, think carefully about how to do it and whether to do it at all. Get it wrong and you sound patronising. Caroline Smith's *The Immigration Handbook* deals powerfully with refugee and immigrant stories.

She does not pretend to be a refugee, but makes found poems out of genuine case notes, changing names to respect privacy.

Get yourself out of the poem if you can. Do you need to say 'I' at all, or can you put someone else at the centre of this issue? The difference between an engaging poem and a patronising one is often ego.

YouTube and vlogging allow you to circulate a topical poem to millions of people before the news story goes cold. Hollie McNish, Dean Atta and Mark Grist have all used social media to spread their message. It's commonly said that our online communities are echo chambers in which we speak only to like-minded people but, as poet Lemn Sissay reminded me, 'Preaching to the converted is not a wasted effort. The converted need to be spoken to as well.' There is value in building solidarity, and letting others who share your views know that they are not alone.

Further reading:

Anna Akhmatova writes about state oppression with steely compassion.
Maya Angelou turns racism and oppression into laughter and strength.
Malika Booker, Warsan Shire and **Sharon Olds** are all found in a new volume from Penguin – *Penguin Modern Poets 3: Your Family, Your Body* which does what it says on the tin.
John Clare – socially engaged poetry is nothing new, as Clare shows in writing of a rural life disrupted by enclosure.
Jim Carruth's book *Black Cart* gives a humane and funny chronicle of dairy farmers, protesting their treatment by successive governments.
Steve Ely and **Ian Duhig** use old traditions and sharp new wit to focus on the present.
Mark Doty's poetry is a great example of the long free-verse American poem.

U A Fanthorpe tackles jobsworth bureaucracy or inequality.

Carolyn Forché writes politically engaged poems on human rights and genocide.

Choman Hardi writes as a Kurdish woman with experience of forced migration.

Seamus Heaney wrote about Northern Ireland with a subtlety for which he was sometimes blamed. **Colette Bryce** writes from the same territory.

Philip Levine, former US Laureate, documents and protests working-class American lives.

Elvis McGonagall is a ranting, comedic satirist.

Hollie McNish's *Nobody Told Me* (Picador) is a diary with poems describing the joy, tiredness and fury of young motherhood. Find her on YouTube.

Kei Miller in *The Cartographer Tries to Map a Way to Zion* (Carcanet) maps Jamaican identity, using registers of language and characterisation.

Adrian Mitchell, Tony Harrison and **Brian Patten** give different approaches to political/ social poetry in the north of England, from the 1960s onwards.

Paul Summers writes of northern English post-industrial life.

Joelle Taylor writes about sexual identity and abuse, working class culture and standing up for women. See her collection *Songs My Enemies Taught Me* (Outspoken Press, 2017).

Lemn Sissay and **Benjamin Zephaniah** write powerfully about young black men in a predominantly white society.

Kate Tempest, in *Let Them Eat Chaos* and other works, charts urban life and hardship.

Gil Scott Heron – *The Revolution Will Not Be Televised* inspired a whole generation of poets.

Tony Walsh's *Sex and Love and Rock'n'Roll* is full of music and social commentary.

Tim Wells is a modern-day Ranter, whose 'Stand Up and Spit' events celebrate punk poetry.

Luke Wright's live shows and publications are amongst the best in modern satire, setting about various targets with surgical precision.

CHAPTER SIXTEEN
How to Explore the World of Poetry Magazines and Journals

Whilst these powerful ideas on poetry-writing percolate, let us take a little step in another direction and start to think about the ways in which poetry starts its journey out into the world.

One of the best things about sending poems out there is that you let them go, *make* them finished, and by this process, make room for more new poems to begin. It's a part of the poetry cycle. Magazines and journals are the usual first-step for most poets looking to get their poetry into print, and will be an important part of the process of building a track record of publication. I will talk more later on about what track record is, and why it matters. For now, let's take a look at the world of the poetry magazine and journal, and find out why it is worth exploring.

Why publish in poetry magazines?
Very simply, getting at least a few poems in magazines or journals (online or in print) in the first instance before starting to submit your poems to publishers is essential. It not only puts your poems before a readership, but it also ensures you can demonstrate to publishers that other editors have already seen merit in your poetry, and that there is already awareness out there (however small-scale) of your poetry.

It is also good practice and a valuable discipline. It will help you to work out where your own poetry sits within the wider poetry landscape and introduce you to your peers, the other fellow fledgling poets who are starting out and getting work picked up in magazines. Getting your poems published means you will also usually be sent a complimentary copy of the magazine, so beyond the satisfaction of seeing your work in print, you'll hopefully make some discoveries and find other writers whose work you enjoy.

How can you tell which magazines are worth having poems published in?

One of the best ways to find out about reputable print and online magazines is to look at the acknowledgements section in poetry books and pamphlets by poets whose work you like, or may have followed a similar trajectory as recently published or emerging names.

The Poetry Library offers a comprehensive list and an archive of the majority of the leading magazines. These resources can be accessed at the library, but can also be accessed online at www.poetrymagazines.org.uk.

The next step is to do some research – subscribe to some magazines or try a sample issue, see what you think to the poems and kinds of poetry they publish.

Value your poems and don't be afraid *not* to submit if you don't think of the quality of the magazine is good enough.

It is worth keeping an eye out for rising or new magazines with a good reputation. These will not yet be as overwhelmed by submissions as some of the more established ones, so you may stand a better chance of having work accepted.

Print vs. Online magazines and journals

There are now many excellent online journals and poetry magazines, and one of the big advantages of having a poem accepted and published online is that it has the potential to reach a far bigger readership, and to remain out there for a much longer period of time. It is also eminently shareable, and gives you the opportunity to link to it from your own blog and share via social media.

There are some drawbacks, of course: not *all* online magazines are equal and there can be some you'd want to avoid. If you're new to the world of poetry, it might seem impossible to know where to start online, and hard to tell the reputable online magazines from the less reputable ones. A few key things you should look out for:

A reputable online poetry magazine will have a submissions process and guidelines like any reputable print magazine. It will also be likely to have named editor(s), and a waiting period whilst your submission is considered. It should also be free of charge to submit to.

Read the poems on the site – are they any good? Never just submit because you think an online magazine (or print magazine, for that matter) doesn't have very high or demanding standards but would easily accept your work. Only send your poems to places you will be proud to have had them placed.

Beware of the kind of poetry websites that are not much more than very basic self-publishing platforms, covered in garish ads and clickbait, and where the editorial quality control is low or non-existent. Your poems aren't submitted or considered by any named editor(s), but rather self-submitted and almost immediately posted online, 'published' at the click of a button, along with thousands of others. Publication here is really unlikely to impress an editor, or find you an audience, beyond the message from a stranger who seems to post a message on every poem on the site, yours included, that reads *'woah sublime words so beautiful wow amazing poetry.'*

Not sure how reputable an online poetry site or e-zine is? Google the names of the poets who have been recently published there – do any of them have proper track records of publication, in magazines, books or pamphlets by publishers whose names you've heard of, or just self-published works or eBooks only? A good, reputable poetry site (like *And Other Poems, New Boots and Pantisocracies, Proletarian Poetry* or *Ink, Sweat and Tears*) will feature poems from up-and-coming or established poets with books or pamphlets out or on their way, and will publish just a few poems at a time, maybe a couple of times a week or a month, not just lots of unknown names being published every hour or so.

✑ Top Tips

As with sending poems in to competitions, it can become an expensive habit to buy or subscribe to lots of poetry magazines. Whilst it's good to support the poetry ecosystem, to keep the cost down you could also:

- Buy single copies first to sample the magazine and see what you think of it first before committing to a subscription.
- Purchase a subscription to different magazines each year, so you get a flavour of the different magazines over time. Ideal Christmas gift suggestion, maybe?
- Club together with a poetry friend or two, and each subscribe to a couple of magazines. You can then swap and share different issues and see which ones might suit you best.

Also, why not give this activity a go:

On your own, or with a poetry friend, do a survey of the poetry magazines you have. Note down the following and report back on your findings on:

- Your first impressions of the magazine, i.e. quality, how it is laid out, what the tone or style is like.
- What kind of writing it seems to contain – do you recognise the names of any of these poets?
- What do you think of the submission guidelines – any queries, are they clear?
- Anything you really like – and which poems do you especially enjoy?
- Anything you don't like or that could be improved? What is off-putting?

CHAPTER SEVENTEEN
On Submitting to Magazines and Journals: The Patented Jo Bell Method

Many people, especially those at the beginning of their writing career, don't have much idea of how to submit work to a poetry journal or what time span is realistic for an editor to consider it. They also wonder how to keep tabs on the seventeen different pieces that they've sent out, or how to avoid the no-no of simultaneous submission, where you send the same piece of work to two or more outlets.

The key part of winning any prize or getting into a journal is this: SEND THE BLIGHTERS OFF. Whilst not everyone who sends work off will get it published, I can guarantee that everyone who gets work published has sent it off. Let's imagine that you are starting this process on January 1st.

January 1st
Make a table or database with four columns:

AVAILABLE	IN CIRCULATION	PUBLISHED	DATE WHEN AVAILABLE AGAIN
Autumn			
Ode to Agatha			
A Sad Lament			
A Journey			

Do it on the computer, because you will be cut-and-pasting from this for years. Put into the first column the titles of all your poems that you think are ready. By the way, they are never ready. You will never send out a poem that you are wholly and perfectly satisfied with. Nobody does. Abandon that hope. Do your best.

January 30th

Make a habit of setting aside one day a month for submissions. Put it in the diary. On the first occasion, take three 'available' poems and send them to Magazine A. Transfer their titles to 'In Circulation'. Send three DIFFERENT ones to Magazine B, three different again to Magazine C, and two or three to Competition X. Put all their titles in the 'In Circulation' column. You're in business. In the 'Date When Available Again' put a date six months from now, or the date when competition results are announced.

AVAILABLE	IN CIRCULATION	PUBLISHED	DATE WHEN AVAILABLE AGAIN
	Autumn (Magma)		
	A Journey (Magma)		
	Ode to Agatha (The Rialto)		
	A Sad Lament (Poetry Review)		

February 28th

Astonishingly, you have not heard a word from Magazine A, B or C. You have been waiting by your inbox like Greyfriars Bobby every morning but still no word. How very odd. Never mind. Send three poems to Magazine D, three to Magazine E, three to Magazine F. Once sent, forget them. They are dead to you until they come back or get accepted.

March 30th

Continue. Never send the same poem to two different magazines or competitions at the same time. This does matter. I nearly lost a very substantial prize once, by doing it accidentally. Editors don't want to slave through a pile of hundreds of poems and accept a handful which they are happy to stand by, only to be told that one of them has just been accepted by a rival magazine. The only reward for editors' labours is that they get to put into print the work they believe in, for the first time. They want to do so without fear of copyright arguments or simple embarrassment. They may have chosen poems to complement each other – your sonnet sitting alongside someone else's, for instance. If you withdraw yours, it will have an impact beyond your own poem and create a space which they have to fill.

Likewise, don't send an email saying 'oh good heavens, I didn't realise it was still with magazine Z because those clowns kept me waiting for so long – I do apologise!' They have heard it before, and are probably about to have dinner with the editor of magazine Z. If your poems are good, they will be accepted eventually, so don't rush it. If they aren't, they won't, so there is nothing to be gained by pushing. Either way, don't submit to two places at once.

April 30th

Etc., etc. You are losing the will to live. You are running out of poems to send out. Fear not, you are about to get some back. Four months is not unusual, six months not unheard of. You might get a response from Magazine A around now if you are lucky. Hurrah, they want one of your poems. It will always be the one you stuck in the envelope last, thinking it was a no-hoper. Send a brief mail saying 'thanks, I'm delighted.' Move the title of that poem into the 'Published' column; buy yourself a new pair of shoes, put down the deposit on that house. Tell everyone on Facebook.

AVAILABLE	IN CIRCULATION	PUBLISHED	DATE WHEN AVAILABLE AGAIN
		Autumn (Magma)	
A Journey			
	Ode to Agatha (Rialto)		
	A Sad Lament (Poetry Review)		

And then put the poems that they *don't* want right back into the 'Available' column. If they don't want any of the poems, no need to reply. If you must, just send them a line saying 'thank you for letting me know, good luck with this issue.' Honestly. That's all.

May 30th

Send out some poems, as usual. If you get an acceptance, hurrah. If you get a rejection, hurrah – you now have some poems free for the next journal or competition, just when you were wondering what to send out. Those which come back, put in the Available folder again, and then send them to magazines that haven't seen them before. Those which are accepted, put in the Published folder. Those which come back over and over again... may need revision. On the balance of probabilities, if nine editors have rejected a poem it is likely not an undiscovered masterpiece, but a poem that needs fixing. Take that as a valuable piece of free feedback. Review, revise, put it back in the Available folder.

AVAILABLE	IN CIRCULATION	PUBLISHED	DATE WHEN AVAILABLE AGAIN
		Autumn (Magma)	
	Ode to Agatha (Rialto)		
	A Sad Lament (Poetry Review)		
	A Journey (National Poetry Competition)		January 30th

Keep sending the blighters off. The editor of Journal F, after all, has very different taste to the editor of Magazine A, and has not seen your poem before. It is fresh as a daisy to her. Remember however, that there is no shortage of daisies in her in-tray. She is eating and drinking poems. She is sick of poems. She wakes up in the night wondering why she does this. Cut her some slack.

Develop a stoical acceptance of the flow – some pieces coming back, some going out, and every now and then a little firework going up to mark a success. Eventually you will be so serene about rejection that you will be quite disappointed when a poem is accepted because this interrupts the endless recycling process.

Continue, ad infinitum. Check the dates in the fourth column of your table every so often. The competition results have been announced and you have inexplicably not won the National Poetry Competition (again)? Those three poems are now free. Put them back in the Available column. Everyone you know who wins competitions, loses competitions too.

Do not (even, indeed especially, while drunk and discouraged) send journals a slightly tetchy email saying 'I haven't heard from you, and I should have thought that four months is quite long enough'. You might perhaps send an email (after six months, not before) saying 'You won't remember my poem *On* 'The Digestive System of the Hippopotamus' – this is just to let you know that there is an RSPCA competition on Pachyderms at the moment, so I'm withdrawing the poem, in the unlikely event that you wanted to use it. Good luck with all your sifting, I know you have a lot of poems to wade through.'

They do. They have a heap of poems as deep as their desk, and they mean no offence by hanging on to yours. They very possibly haven't read it yet. They certainly have a lot of other poems (more than you imagine, and by better poets than you think) to consider. They have poems piled up in the lounge, the bathroom, the bedside table. Their partners already think they spend too much time on this. The work is not only unpaid, but they have to scrabble for funding to keep the magazine afloat at all. It is stressful and almost entirely unrewarding. They have day jobs, often running small poetry presses which make them just enough money to pay the bills if they are lucky. Like you, they have children and social lives and commitments. Like you, they are trying to write their own works of genius and (possibly unlike you) they are also putting something back into the poetry ecosystem. They get ten or twenty notes a week from sensitive souls saying 'I sent you my poem last Tuesday and am exceedingly surprised that you have not yet replied to it. You will be sorry when I win the Pulitzer Prize.' They feel bad about this. They dread going to book launches because someone who has a grudge against them, for rejecting a poem which they don't even remember, will say something snide about the time it takes them to reply. The only reward for all this is that occasionally they get to put into print someone whose work they love. It might be you. It might not.

I'm not putting the editor on a pedestal – but remember that in this process, you are the supplicant. The editor has more poems than s/he knows what to do with. No matter how great your unrecognised genius, indeed no matter how great your recognised genius, editors are doing you a favour by considering your poem. They will not remember your name as one of the dozens of poems on their bedside table – but believe me, they will remember it (immediately, and for a long time) if you join the ranks of the narky, sarky and unpleasant who bitched about their response times.

Set up that database or table and get started. Gradually you will start to accumulate titles in the Published column, but there will always be a lot more titles in the Available column.

If you're disheartened by that, then it may be that you're looking for an excuse to be disheartened. Really, it is not so hard to put a poem in an envelope or send it by email and then forget about it. And it really does get easier, the more you do it.

CHAPTER EIGHTEEN
How to Submit Your Poems

Much of what Jo and I share with you in *How to be a Poet* is about demystifying the various aspects of poetry. One area that seems to cause a great deal of confusion and conflagration is the topic of submitting poetry, so we're keen to ensure plenty of detailed advice and first- hand experience here.

In addition to Jo's patented method for submissions, I'm going to share a bit of a peek behind the scenes into the editor's submissions pile, and tell you about some of the submissions that get it very wrong, so that you can be prepared to get it very right when you send your poems off. Much of this advice applies to both submitting poetry manuscripts and submitting to magazines, though some points may also be more pertinent to different types of submission than others.

Over the last decade, I've gathered a selection of cautionary tales about poetry submissions. There was the poet who sent me their auntie's letter of endorsement for their poetry (full and unexpurgated, including some quite personal family gossip). There was the angry poet who sent me a tirade after I rejected their manuscript: *'you'd have probably turned down The Beatles and The Rolling Stones too'*. Or the poet who sent me one long poem written in pencil in very tiny handwriting on a scroll of paper (which, due to lack of correct postage, I'd also had to visit the sorting office to collect and pay to retrieve. I wasn't best pleased by the time I prised open that envelope to find the very tiny poems enclosed therein).

You, dear reader, are already far more sensible than these poets, who have it so badly wrong they are unlikely to find a publisher. You are, after all, reading this book and trying to find out the best way to go about things. Sometimes, poets worry too much that they'll get the submission wrong, and for a tiny error will have their work rejected. That's rarely the case.

If you're worrying like this, you're already concerned with getting it right, which is a pretty important and positive step.

I regularly encounter people who believe earnestly that the rules and requests around submission is nit-picking etiquette designed to keep virtuosos and geniuses at bay by the dullards of a publishing industry who wouldn't recognise their true talent if it leapt out at them dressed as Thomas Hardy's belligerent but rather sad ghost. The more boring reality is that the rules in submission guidelines are there to help editors and publishers manage the flow of submissions they receive and to try and not waste too much time trying to find out what they need to know, which is generally, *do I want to publish this, or not?*

There's not much we can do if a writer already has this kind of mindset, but we can at least learn from some of their errors and be sure not to commit them ourselves. In addition, there are plenty of less critical but more common pitfalls that poets fall into when sending out their work.

Here are some of the things you should definitely NOT do when sending out your poems:

Send your poems out to multiple editors, all at once, in a mass email. Editors will know when someone has done this as we can see all the other publishers and magazine editors cc'd into the email. And if you've blind copied them in, we've already clocked the 'unspecified recipients' and are suspicious of your generic email template that doesn't seem to mention any editor or single publisher by name. Approach only one publisher at a time; it isn't an auction where your poems will be snapped up by the highest bidder.

Send out simultaneous submissions. I'm often asked why simultaneous submissions are an issue, and for me it's about time, patience and respect. If I've wasted time reading and longlisting and then shortlisting your poems for a magazine or competition, I'm not going to be quite so happy to find they have already been accepted elsewhere. I may have already made the final choices, and rejected everyone else, so it may not be possible to offer the opportunity to someone else. The same goes for submitting your poems and then withdrawing them because they've been accepted elsewhere. This does causes wasted reading-time, and suggests that the poet in question is impatient to have their work taken at any price. Try to be patient. Poetry is, for better or worse, a slow art and a slow-moving world. Take your time, and the successes will feel all the more rewarding for it.

Send your self-published book of poems. I was once sent two lavishly produced hardback copies of a self-published book by a writer, with postage that had cost them dearly and a note enquiring if I'd consider publishing this book. I wonder how many other publishers this book had been sent to? The cost of publishing and sending it out must have run into many hundreds of pounds, and possibly even more than that. I felt sorry that this writer had done this, but it was too late to advise them not to. Sadly, no publisher will accept or publish work sent to them in a self-published book. You have already just published it, and possibly also assigned it an ISBN, so our job has already been done.

Submit anything other than your poems and a simple covering letter. Unless specifically requested, all that your submission should contain is a short covering letter (with a biography and some brief background information if it is a manuscript submission for a collection and pamphlet) and the poems themselves. Do not send photographs, lengthy CVs, CDs or memory cards, long letters of endorsement or any other item. Keep it simple and only send what has been asked for. If you're not too sure what a covering letter should ideally look like or contain, read on, as I will give an example in Chapter Twenty-Four.

Send your submission even when the publisher or magazine is not open to submissions. This tells the editor you've either not read their submissions guidelines, and gone straight to the 'Contact' page of their website (and ignored the note there that asks you not to send submissions by email), or you have seen both, and decided to send your work anyway, unsolicited. Either way, it is unlikely to get you in an editor's good books – remember that open submissions reading windows are there to allow publishers to manage the flow of the work they receive so that they have time to consider and make decisions. Some publishers will be open to submissions all year round, but others will have calls for submissions, and the majority of magazines will have dates when they are open to submissions or closed. Abide by the rules, and don't ignore the preference of each publisher.

Put copyright symbols on your submission. There is no need to do this and it makes a submission look amateurish.

Demand feedback on a submission. Most editors will not be able to give feedback on submissions to magazines or to their publishing list, due to the large volume of submissions they receive. I do sometimes get asked to read and give feedback on a submission, and I will almost always decline. To give proper, genuine feedback is a time-consuming activity that involves a day, at least, with a manuscript. It involves care and input, and a sense that the advice is right for the poet at that stage and will be received in the spirit in which it is given. In the case of manuscript feedback, it is also additional work for which an editor is not being paid, and for which someone who does offer this service professionally is not being paid either. Ultimately, the rejection of the work *is* my feedback – *this isn't for me, sorry.*

If you do want to get in-depth feedback on your poems, I do recommend other methods – The Literary Consultancy (TLC) offers high-quality manuscript assessments by published poets and editors, generally in the form of a written report which will give detailed feedback and realistic advice. For low-income writers, they also currently offer the TLC Free Reads scheme, supported by Arts Council England. In addition, The Poetry School has a list of poetry mentors if you think that this route may be of use before you send work out (see our appendix for the useful link to the website). The Poetry School also offer tutorials, manuscript assessments, mentoring arrangements and run an online fortnightly feedback course once a term. Though they do not currently offer concessions or bursaries on one-to-one work, they are available for all their courses, so do consider applying if eligible. It's worth keeping an eye out for other courses or workshops designed to give feedback on manuscripts or poetry, and also for one-to-one advice sessions or writer's surgeries that are on offer with editors at some festivals and conferences. Join email lists for news and information from your local literature development agency.

Did you know that individual writers can apply for Arts Council funding grants to develop and support their work? You can use the funding to pay for your writing time, a mentor's expertise, a writing course or feedback on your manuscript. See the useful links again at the back of this book for further information.

Sometimes, if I know a submission is *almost* there, or might suit another publisher better, I may include this encouragement in my reply to the poet, or some brief feedback, but I can rarely give this on demand. If you **do** get feedback from a magazine or journal on a rejection slip or email (i.e. 'liked your seagull poem but sadly couldn't take any this time'), count this as a really good and encouraging sign. You should probably consider sending work again to the magazine in future. You should also perhaps send that seagull poem out somewhere else – clearly, it's struck a chord.

Send the same manuscript or poems back to the same publisher. It is rare for a publisher to want to reconsider a submission they've rejected – so don't resubmit the same manuscript or poems again unless specifically encouraged or advised to by the editor.

Chase a status update. I do sometimes receive emails from very eager poets – it's been a few days since our suggested response period has passed and they are already writing to ask if I've reached a decision or not. Trouble is, if I receive a lot of these, I can easily spend a good chunk of time I'd have spent reading the submissions responding to these emails instead. Whilst it's great to be keen, badgering editors and magazines for a decision is not helpful.

Of course, if an editor or magazine has been too long with your submission (a few months more than suggested, for instance) do give them a gentle nudge. And if your enquiry doesn't elicit a response, or if you are left dangling again for a month or two, it is absolutely reasonable to write and withdraw the poems and take them somewhere else.

Send submissions, emails or letters addressed 'Dear Sirs'. This is outdated, rude and unnecessary and is a really good way to guarantee a very short trip from an editor's in-tray to the bin. Perhaps this sounds a little brutal, but why should an editor wish to publish (and, in effect, work with) someone who not only can't be bothered to find out their name and address a letter to them personally, but assumes everyone who works in publishing is a man? Equally, if a magazine has a two editors, please don't address your submission to the male editor only (yes, people really *do* do this).

Send angry responses to a rejection. It is never a great feeling to have your work rejected, and it isn't something that an editor takes any pleasure in doing. Even now, I still dislike the process of turning down manuscripts and poems, so I try to make the process as painless as possible for both parties. The only response to a rejection is perhaps to thank the editors for their time in considering and responding to your work. Editors may sometimes have terrible memories, but are strangely good at recalling the names of those who have sent rude emails following a rejection – or posted an angry response to their work being declined on their social media or blog.

And here are some useful, positive things you should definitely DO:

Your research. Save yourself time and energy by making sure you know where your work is best situated in the wider poetry landscape – and who publishes what. There is no point sending a submission that clearly isn't suited to the publisher in question, i.e. you wouldn't send radical experimental urban poetry to a magazine that tends to only publish traditional sonnets and nature themed eco-poetry.

No one expects you to fit into a pigeon hole (and I like surprising and challenging new work as much as the next editor) but you should feel a little confident that the work you are presenting to the publisher isn't too far removed from the kind of poetry their list showcases. Also, do you like the kind of books this publisher produces, or enjoy this particular magazine? If not, why are you submitting your work to them?

Read the guidelines and stick to them. You want an editor to be on your side before they even see the first poem. By submitting your poems correctly, in the manner in which an editor prefers to receive them, you ensure the only thing they will notice is the poetry itself. Make a good impression from the first step.

Address the submission correctly. It does make a good impression if you address your submission to the editor(s) personally by name if you can – if you can't then simply 'Dear Editor(s)' is perfectly acceptable. Using names shows the publisher you have taken the time and effort to check the website or submissions information carefully, and spent some time getting to know the magazine or press, and the kind of poetry they tend to publish.

Ask if you're not sure. Editors don't bite (well, most of us don't, anyway...) and we are usually more than happy to answer a query. In fact, I've often found it useful in the past when people have asked questions as it's helped me to make my guidelines clearer. I'd far rather you ask than assume and get it horribly wrong.

CHAPTER NINETEEN
Why Publish Your Poetry?
by Clive Birnie

If someone drops a poem in the forest – and no one picks it up and reads it – is the writer a poet? Are you a poet if your poetry exists only on the hard disk of your laptop?

There are many reasons to seek publication. Validation. Critical adulation. Money, money, money. All are possible although not necessarily equally attainable. I think it is important to think about your motives and direction before you start. To ask yourself *why* you are submitting poetry for publication. The most obvious reason for most of us is validation that the poetry we are writing is poetry that others will want to read and, most importantly, that editors will consider worthy of publication. For the new poet, there is a golden moment when that first acceptance comes back. It is a good feeling. You can finally update your online profile with the word... poet.

There are different roads to that moment. Some journal editors will say read our back issues, send us something similar. That is a tight brief, and not one I personally like, but many a poet has made their way by piling up a considerable CV of individually published poems. Some book publishers like to see this before they consider a poet ready to publish a collection. I personally see this as kind of old school and suspect many of the newer generation of small press editors feel the same. We'd rather hear your voice and crave the poetry that stands out from the herd.

This points to the alternative option: write what you want, the way you want and then doggedly seek out the right places to submit to get that first success. But let me take you back a step and ask you again why you want to be published? What is the mission? What are your goals? Oh I know, I hate being asked this as well, but hear me out. If you hold the ambition and self-belief to think that your poetry might one day be in competition for a small, medium or major prize, where you start is relevant. Starting out in slams and pursuing a career in what is currently labelled 'spoken word' will not help. All poetries are not equal. If you want to win a jazz award, don't play heavy metal. If you want critical acclaim there are few options (the literary review is dead) and you will need to catch the eye of the bigger presses. You will need someone else to advise how to achieve that. Every press, every editor has their own set of guidelines and rules. Read them. Absorb them. Follow them.

Publication is not the only option, of course. You have the astonishing good fortune to be here in the twenty-first century. Not so long ago, the only option for the apprentice poet was to stuff envelopes with paper and post them out into dead letter boxes. Now armed with your digital device of choice and a Submittable account the world is at your keyboard. But slow down... what else does that digital device offer? How else might you distribute your work? Who reads poetry 'zines and journals anyway? Turn on – sign in – upload. Sit back and count the likes of that film-poem you just shot and edited on your phone. There are film-poets and instapoets carving out decent careers for themselves having never read or considered the legacy alternatives of the paper-laden past. Not to mention the spoken word poets who might have a decade of performance behind them before considering publication and perhaps only embracing it in the end when they realise the financial potential of the poetry book as merchandise.

Which segues neatly into the dirty dark secret of poetry-book publishing: you will sell most of the copies of your book yourself. Aside from a few notable exceptions most new poetry books barely trouble the inside of a bookshop never mind break through to the Bookseller / Nielsen charts, but poets get booked for festivals, readings, workshops, gigs and that means they get to hand-sell books to the people they meet and get to keep the biggest slug of margin for themselves. Margin? Yep, margin – the difference between the money you take and the cost of you buying a copy from your publisher. If a bookshop sells a book they take a cut, and then there is a wholesaler, a distributor, a sales agency, all taking a slice. You might get a royalty payment six months later... if you are lucky. Or you can sell a book to an audience member at an event and put that £10 note in your pocket – pay the publisher what you owe and keep the share that the bookshops and co. would have eaten.

The best-selling poets I know are their own bookshop, have their own online store and never go to an event without a box of books. They are business-like about being artists and see publication as an essential facet of the economic model that maintains their independence to live the creative life. If you asked me to cut this back to single reason why you should take publication seriously – that would be it.

Clive Birnie comes from a long line of drowned Peterhead fisherman, but lives on a hill above the Severn Sea where the siren of Blacknore Point can be heard and evidence of a medieval tsunami can be found in the geology of the shore. He is co-owner and trouble-maker in chief at Burning Eye Books.

CHAPTER TWENTY
How to Polish your Manuscript for Publication: Part One

Though Jo has already thoroughly covered redrafting your individual poems, I'd like to take you through the final steps towards polishing a whole manuscript or manuscript sample before submitting it to an editor. I hope here to offer some advice which will help you to become your own best self-editor, and provide you with skills which will be rewarding and useful in all your future poetry endeavours.

This final stage of redrafting and editing is a process of developing your own confidence and being able to objectively look at your own poems in order to fix the problems within them. The more that you understand *what* makes a good poem tick, (by reading and writing as much as you can), and are able to apply it to your own work, the more you will also feel confident in knowing what you need to do to make your own poems watertight and ship-shape. Much of this is instinctive; it is about learning to trust your instincts about what a poem needs to make it the best it can be.

This does not happen overnight, so don't worry if you still feel you lack some confidence in editing your poems. Workshops can help reshape and get new perspectives on your poetry. A residential writing course can be useful, as can joining other workshops or one-to-one sessions where you can get creative and helpful feedback. But the good news is that there is also a lot you can do for yourself as a confident self-editor.

Here are a few of my key tips for refining, editing and putting the final polish on your work before you start sending it out:

Proofread your poems. By this, I mean that you should not just rely on the spellcheck to get things right. Spellcheck will often miss typos and won't help you to identify places where your writing doesn't make sense or the punctuation isn't working to help make your poems clear. Print out and read your poems with care, and read them in different orders (the eye becomes over-familiar to reading things in the same order, and more likely to miss mistakes). If in doubt, ask someone else to read and check them for you.

Read aloud in private at home, and if possible do 'road-test' your poems publicly if you can find a friendly and supportive open mic evening where you feel happy to read aloud. Be attentive to the sounds and shapes of the poems as you read – is anything standing out as difficult to read? Are you feeling a bit breathless? Is the punctuation helping you to read or getting in the way? Adjust as you need to. Your poem will be read aloud in the readers' mind, so if it's not working when *you* read aloud, it is likely your readers also will also struggle.

Remember that punctuation is like the musical notation of a poem – it should tell the reader where to breathe, where to pause, where to take it slowly or speed up. It controls the reading as well as the meaning. Don't assume a reader will know how to read a poem if your punctuation isn't helping them. If it isn't quite working for you when you read aloud, go back and take a much closer look at what your commas, colons, semi-colons, dashes and full stops are really doing.

Prune anything that doesn't earn its place. Be brave and don't be frightened of trimming poems right back. Make every single word work hard to earn its place. If something feels a bit out of shape or not quite working, make sure you look closely and consider if it really needs to be in the poem. I often tell my students and mentees that a good poem is like a Jenga tower – you've taken away as much unnecessary material as you dare, without making the whole thing sway or become unstable – the poem is perfectly poised, balanced *just so.*

Be honest about your faults and bad habits. Make a list of some of these. Are there certain words you overuse, do you find poem titles tricky, or maybe line breaks and punctuation are your main problem? If so, by acknowledging and identifying problems, you can look at the poems with a slightly more detached view. Identify similar faults in other poems, and work to fix them. If you overuse certain words or themes, you may also be able to find the poems where these words work and are integral (and need to stay) but also the places where you could refresh the poem and do something different. Be challenging to yourself, especially where you sense you may be getting a bit too comfortable or not pushing your work to be as original as it could be.

Why not pin this list somewhere prominent when you write, so you're conscious of looking out for these bad habits when you come around to redrafting?

Watch out for 'telling' rather than 'showing'. Ask yourself: are you just 'telling' the reader what to think – reporting or instructing as if it's simply a status update or a news report? Or are you creating a scene, where the reader is invited in, encouraged to deploy their imagination and join the dots and make a connection to your writing by reaching an understanding of what you are suggesting?

Spot the cliché. Comb through every poem carefully for clichés, and remove them where you find them. Your own thoughts will always be better than ready-made ones. Cliché will make your work seem much less original, and one cliché can really make an otherwise excellent poem seem weaker. George Orwell (in his brilliant essay, 'Politics and the English Language') cautions against cliché and the danger of 'the ready-made phrases', which 'will construct your sentences for you – even think your thoughts for you, to a certain extent – and at need they will perform the important service of partially concealing your meaning even from yourself.'

Choose good titles. As Jo has also explored, a dull or boring title can critically undersell your poems. A title which also doesn't fit with the poem, is too strange or jokey, or doesn't really help the reader to understand the poem may be problematic. A title is a true multi-tasker. It is more than simply a descriptor to separate one poem from another. A title can be a subtle device to explain or illuminate the reader. It can also be a source of interest or intrigue ('what's this all about?') or may even be a ploy or a trick, a way of toying with the reader's expectations and then subverting them. The title is not a separate thing from the poem – it is an integral part of the poem.

What does your title bring to the poem – does it work in unison with the poem, in juxtaposition or in tension with it? Does it bring a new angle, or provide the essential key to unlocking the poem's meaning? The same also applies to poetry collection and pamphlet titles.

Keep your own little store of poem and collection titles, things that pop into your head and would be easily lost – jot them on your phone or in a notebook. When you have time, use these for writing exercises. You never know when a great title might help you to write that poem you've been trying to get started for a long time.

Paying your dues: do make sure you credit any debts you have to other writers or artists. By this, we mean that you acknowledge any quotes in your poems, influences, or bits you may have 'borrowed'.

If you have borrowed *anything* at all from another poet's poem and used it to structure, inform or inspire your own be VERY clear that you acknowledge your debt to their original work. The usual way to do this is to include 'After…' under your poem's title, i.e. 'After Langston Hughes' to acknowledge this. You may also want to consider adding a footnote if relevant, or putting it in the acknowledgments of your manuscript if you've used a specific form or structure or lines from a specific poem as your jumping-off point.

The same goes for 'found' poems, or poems that use newspapers, essays, Wikipedia entries etc. Please be aware of exactly what plagiarism is and make sure you always give credit and acknowledgment wherever it is due.

✍ Top Tips

The showing-not-telling exercise

I use this workshop exercise to illustrate exactly what the difference is between a line that 'tells' the reader and one which 'shows'. Bear in mind these are for illustrative purposes only, and are not meant as examples of well-written poetry!

To have a go at this exercise yourself, make a photocopy of this table opposite, and cut up the phrases onto strips of paper. Lay them out and match up the example 'telling' phrase to its partner 'showing' version.

In the city the sun is shining so it is very hot and I am sweating.	A melancholy loss, this gap, absence.
I feel really happy when we are together.	In the deep, steep, wooded heart of home.
He is an angry man who shouts and swears a lot.	Wind-toppled oaks and beech trees litter parkland like dominoes.
I feel so sad that someone has died.	Circling in and spying from steep thermals, wing-tips wide.
Terry is a brilliant musician, he can play guitar well and practises a lot.	I glitter in the spotlight of your company.
The eagle is flying very high up and is looking for prey.	My clothes stick to me in the bright, white-hot streets.
She is thinking about her son who lives far away and worries about him.	Shivering, mud-covered flanks, the fly-eyed lonely mare.
The place where I live is very hilly and there is a lot of woodland nearby.	His worn fingers pluck the strings, refrains bright and alive.
The horse is not well cared for and the farmer neglects it.	He is a bad-tempered blizzard.
After a very windy storm, the trees in the park had blown over.	She draws the dots of distance, imagines where or how he is.

CHAPTER TWENTY-ONE
On Getting it Wrong

'Pretty much everyone in every profession outside of professional athletics gets better as they go along, for the rather obvious reason that they learn and they practise. Why should writers be different?'
– Mark Forsyth, *The Elements of Eloquence*

What if everyone else is competent and you're doing it wrong? In this respect, poetry is like parenthood. You *are* doing it wrong; at least, you will always feel that you are. There will never be a time when you feel completely confident with your writing, completely sure that you are expressing yourself perfectly (and if you do, you need to push yourself a little harder). You always feel that you could do it a little bit better.

There are two consolations for this. Firstly, every other writer also feels that they are getting it wrong. I promise you this is true. Secondly, 'getting it wrong', by which we mean 'not writing as well as you want to', is the only way to get it right. That feeling of 'could do better' is precisely what drives us to keep writing. The occasional feeling of failure is honestly a part of creative success. Writers don't always allow for the necessity of this. So you keep imagining that everyone else knows how to do it; they are the real thing, you are a fraud. Nonsense. Keep writing.

Here's a typical experience. You write two poems in a row and they are both, you feel sure, *rubbish*. They seem cliché-ridden; they don't scan properly. The form doesn't sit well with the content, and can you get away with that dodgy rhyme in line 12? (The answer is NO, by the way. In asking the question, you admit to a weakness that needs fixing. Fix it.) Your thoughts as you put down your pen or close the screen are something like this:

I don't know why I do this. Poet Z has just published three brilliant pieces in *The Rialto* magazine, while my work is derivative and trite (or worse still, 'Poet Z has just published three dreadful pieces in *The Rialto* and I am sure I could do better'). I can't even remember what a trochee is. There is no point in submitting my work to journals, when people like Poet Z are effortlessly churning out the sort of thing that editors clearly want. S/he is on a higher plane. I am never going to get noticed. I was foolish to ever think... etc etc.

We'll talk elsewhere about success and what it means. For now, forget about Poet Z or any other poet. They are not in the room, and you are. This thing is important to you, or you wouldn't be tying yourself in knots of self-loathing. Eliminate all thoughts of writing a poem that will win the competition or be published in a journal. Set your course according to your own lights, not someone else's. Never mind that the current fashion is for poems in couplets, or poems about unicorns, or poems about immigration, when you want to write about dragonflies or sawdust. Draw on what you know: from reading, from writing and most importantly from the day-to-day business of living. Then sit down and write your third poem.

This one comes more quickly. You catch hold of a thread that could run through the whole piece and give it structure. You see swiftly that the first half of the poem is waffle and can be cut. You realise that the title doesn't add to the poem, and fix it. The last phrase is too dogmatic so you strike it out to leave an ambivalent ending which will hold the reader's interest all day. You identify the centre of the poem, which is not at all where you thought it was.

You're writing. Look, no hands.

It is not an accident that the third poem is better than the first or second. The third poem is better *because of* the first and second ones. Every poem you write includes a lesson learned from every poem you ever wrote. None of this effort is wasted. Poetry is an art form, and it deserves attention and effort. As the social historian and broadcaster Stuart Maconie says:

People wouldn't say if they found a violin in the street, 'Oh, I think I'll have a go at writing a symphony.' But they think that because they can speak English, they should be able to write without practice and honing their craft.

He doesn't mean *you*, obviously. You're reading this book, in hopes of honing your craft. It's fashionable amongst people who have already achieved a high level of craft, to pretend that it's all natural and that craft doesn't figure in their writing. That's disingenuous. Practice may not make perfect, but it certainly helps you to keep your skills sharp – so that next time you need the writerly toolbox, it's full of well-maintained tricks.

Don't worry about Poet Z. Other poets' success does not diminish yours. Your work only has to be the best you can write, right now. And you can look up *trochee* on the internet any time you need to know.

People crucify themselves with anxiety in trying to get it right. If you've identified poetry writing as an important part of your life, then of course it matters that you do it as well as you can. Ironically, however, that can be the biggest obstacle to actually doing it. I speak as one who knows. A year from now, you'll still feel that you aren't getting it right because you will have moved on, and found new aims or directions. In short, the goalposts will move because you move them. Our ambitions change as time goes on. Perhaps you have had a transforming illness, or seen an exhibition which fed into new artistic appetites. You read a very good poem (perhaps even by that bastard Z) which gave you new insight into your own practice.

On the days when you feel that you will never attain the great heights of Walt Whitman, Marianne Moore or Jean 'Binta' Breeze, remember that all the poems that you so admire in journals or books are the *finished product*. You haven't seen the drafts that the poet worked through to get to the version they finally published. If you constantly compare your early drafts with the finished product of a long-established practitioner, then of course you will feel inferior. Remind yourself of Arthur Ashe's very useful maxim: 'Start where you are. Use what you have. Do what you can.'

In their book *Art & Fear,* David Bayles and Ted Orland tell the apocryphal story of a ceramics teacher who divides his class into two groups. Half of the class are to be graded on quantity – the more pots they produce, the better their marks will be. The other half will be marked on quality. These students can make just one pot, and they'll be given an A grade – so long as it is perfect:

> Came grading time and a curious fact emerged: the works of highest quality were all produced by the group being graded for quantity. It seems that while the 'quantity' group was busily churning out piles of work – and learning from their mistakes – the 'quality' group had sat theorising about perfection, and in the end had little more to show for their efforts than grandiose theories and a pile of dead clay.

Sit down and write. Start again, with Poem Number 199.

✍ Top Tips

Exercise: Return to an early poem
Look at one of the first poems you wrote. Don't edit or change it; just look at it really closely and note in your mind what you would do differently now.

Your early poem will probably make you wince slightly, because you included something that you would now leave out. Perhaps it includes a long preamble, or three splendidly florid adjectives which you find a bit embarrassing now. The object is not to make you beat yourself up for past foolishness but to congratulate yourself on present practice. If you can see that these things don't work, then you have made some progress; and you made that progress by writing this poem, amongst others.

CHAPTER TWENTY-TWO
How to Polish your Manuscript: Part Two

Now, this manuscript of yours is coming along apace and looking good, so let us return to where we left on in my previous chapter. You've deleted the clichés and road-tested the poems, and spotted that terrible typo that crept into the third draft. These poems are sounding clear and distinctive when you read them, and you're ready to start formally bringing the pamphlet or collection of poems together as a final version of the manuscript.

At this crucial stage, there may be a few issues arising; how to order these poems, do the poem's themes matter, and what should go into the final draft of your manuscript?

On themes

I'm often asked how you should go about ordering a manuscript, if a poetry collection should have a theme, and if themed poetry manuscripts are more likely to be published. I think that what the poet may mean by this, and what the publisher will mean are often two separate things – there are the common themes that will exist on the surface (or just beneath) of most good manuscripts. There are also the strands of themes a publisher may pull out of a manuscript they've accepted for publication when they start to think about how they'll market it. There is a close relationship, and plenty of crossover between the two, but the main one for you as poet to consider is the former, the themes which already sit within your poems or your wider body of work.

Generally, what appears to be a random assortment of poems on random topics (a sort of poetry pick 'n' mix) will be a disadvantage at the manuscript stage, especially if there is a sense that this is a collection where the poems feel more like workshop exercises than a coherent whole, lacking some form of thread that may link them together. This is not, however, to say that publishers only seek heavily-themed or structured collections for publication. Rather, it's to say that a well-ordered manuscript that seeks to make connections and draw together subtle themes will stand a far better chance of success. *What* goes in, and the order they go in, will matter in terms of creating a sense of themes threaded through a selection of poems.

My key advice is that all the best collections have something that will be on a spectrum somewhere between a subtle or very a strong or more formal thematic basis. And you must find the right position for you. For instance, you may write on a variety of topics (dogs, libraries, tea and mythology), but your poems may have the common theme of unrequited love. Or perhaps even loss (if it's lost dogs, lost library books, and cold tea…). It's up to the selection and order of poems (and the manuscript's title) to make this clear to the reader – to create a narrative, however loosely, even if one wasn't necessarily there consciously or obviously when the poems were first written. It's all in the compiling.

There are many well-known collections of poetry that operate around one key narrative thread that creates the theme and also influences the poem's form and sequencing; think of Jackie Kay's *Adoption Papers* or Kei Miller's *The Cartographer Tries to Map a Way to Zion*. If you have a story to tell, or a particular theme that really matters to you, it may well emerge as both the structuring device (demanding that the poems appear in a certain order) and the strong narrative arc of the manuscript, driving it onwards, deciding clearly what will go where, chronologically or otherwise.

Equally, a central idea or concept may have formed the heart of your collection, and act as a structuring device – for instance Carol Ann Duffy's *The World's Wife*, or *Dart* by Alice Oswald. Or, if a book takes its cue from a previous work of literature or art, like Patience Agbabi's *Telling Tales* (a modern retelling of Chaucer's *Canterbury Tales*) it will ground itself in (and grow out of) the work that has inspired it.

131

These aren't the only ways to work with themes. Many other poetry books and pamphlets will take on more than one theme through a variety of different poems, or work with theme(s) that are slippery, shape-shifting or subtle. A book of poems that ranges across topics such as museums, lost property, growing up and leaving a hometown could present poems that all take various slants, forms and approaches, but you could sum up its thematic heart as being centred simply on 'grief' or 'love' in a subtle and careful way.

The theme is something that could (and *should* – it's good practice to think about this, as it will help you to establish it clearly for yourself) be summed up simply in a few words, a short sentence. For instance, I remember summing up a certain poet's book as being all about 'Sex, boats and friendship – and yet so much more'. How fitting then that such a book drew itself around a one-word title, *Kith*, to be clear and definite about the various themes it had woven together?

In summary – yes, themes *do* matter. But I'm keen that fledgling poets do not develop an anxiety (particularly around the first collection) that it MUST be heavily, obviously or very formally-themed as if it is a project. A book or pamphlet of poems doesn't have to be written solely or strictly on one theme to be successful, though you have the freedom to do so if you wish, and what is most important is that you write about what really matters to you, and not what you think a publisher or readership wants or expects you to write about.

Selecting what goes in

The poems: first of all, make sure you have enough of a wider body of work to be building a collection. This isn't the total number of poems you've ever written, but rather a selection of the very best ones only; the ones that you feel are as close to finished as they can be, and which might work cohesively together. You might have over 100 poems, but realistically only half of those that you'd want to longlist as possible for a manuscript. As a rough guideline, you should have 18-25 poems for a pamphlet, 40-50 poems for a full collection. If you don't feel there are enough, or you find yourself trying to shoehorn poems in or write into gaps, it may not be quite yet the right time to be pulling the manuscript together. Don't rush. Ask yourself, if one small set of poems feels ready, whether these may be better placed as a pamphlet? Or, (especially if there seems further development to do around the ideas your poems present) you might want to consider whether you should hold onto them for now and let a full collection develop more solidly around this core of poems. Do not simply write more poems for the sake of it; I do sometimes get submissions where the poet has written additional poems specifically to meet the requirements for a collection. These collections are very rarely successful, and the poems written-to-order will stand out as uneven or unconvincing.

Ordering your poems

If you are submitting a manuscript of a pamphlet or book, you will no doubt have begun to wrestle with the ordering of your poems. Questions about ordering often come up in workshops, and I'd suggest that each manuscript will be unique in the kind of order or structure that will work. One of the best pieces of advice I can give you is to do some research and look at how other poets have ordered their books and pamphlets successfully and creatively (see the activity suggested at the end of this chapter for more).

All good books need a beginning, middle and end, so let's think first about this. Where do you want your reader to begin, and what point do you want them to work towards? Is there a title poem, and does this need to be prominently placed? Sometimes, choosing your opening and closing poems can be vital in working out the first framework around which the rest of manuscript can be arranged. Once you've chosen opening and closing poems, you can work backwards and forwards at once, choosing second and penultimate poems, and so on, until a working order emerges.

Consider next not just the overall trajectory of your manuscript from beginning to end, but the small arcs and narratives in between – regard these as the 'chapters' of your manuscript. Breaking the manuscript down into these smaller clusters of poems can help you get the order right within these smaller groupings. As we've mentioned before, you don't need to put poems all on the same theme together, but you may think about the movements of time, ideas and moods in your book and how to find commonalities or contrasts, and arrange these accordingly.

Some poetry collections will have very distinct sections (which might be named or simply numbered), others will work as one cohesive whole with themes changing and coming and going in a more subtle way. Think about what will work best for your manuscript. Do you want the reader to travel though the book with themes drifting, returning and reoccurring? Or do you feel that distinct sets of poems work best together by being grouped? Is there a story or conclusion of some form that it is important, however loosely, which the poems work towards?

Get an overview

It can be useful to print out your poems and lay them out on the floor or on a table. This does mean you can get a visual and physical overview of how the poems work beside each other, and try out different groupings and orders. If this isn't possible, you could use post-it notes with the titles of each poem written on, or summarise them in a line or two ('the poem about cats and ex boyfriends' etc., see the activity that follows in our Top Tips section next). Put the post-its on a wall and move them about, making groups and changing them around until they work.

Identify the weak links

Once you have a rough running order for your collection, look at the flow between the selections of poems you have. Do some now stand out, or seem not to be quite as good as other poems? Are some poems saying the same thing – just saying it more or less successfully? Don't be afraid to pull out these poems and give them two chances. Revise them by trying something radical (i.e. a new poetic form, restructuring the poem etc.) or put them away in a drawer where you will either come back to them in time or conclude they are best left there.

Pick only your best poems

Strive to only put in your very best work. Don't be tempted to bolster a poetry submission with too much 'filler' – poems that you know are okay but only that. It is better to have a shorter, sharper collection or pamphlet, than one with too many so-so poems. An editor will spot the make-weight poems very quickly and it will undermine the strength of the rest of your poems.

✍ Top Tips

Exercise: Form an editorial team

In this exercise, you'll need to find a trusted critical buddy or two, and form an editorial team. In your group or pair, look at some existing poetry collections and study the techniques and structures at work within them. Always learn from the best, and the poets who have been there before you. This is also an exercise you can do by yourself, but it might be more enjoyable and raise more counterpoints and debate over a good cup of tea with your trusty poetry friends.

In your editorial team:

- Look at the titles of the poetry collections on your bookshelves. How do these titles shape your impression of the book? What entices you in, is memorable, or puts you off? What kind of title is right for you?
- Pick three single-author poetry collections at random by different poets and open each one on the contents page. Pick a poem from each to read purely based on the title

– does it live up to or subvert its title? Make a note of how the various titles and poems work together – how are they functioning, and what can you learn from these titles and how they interact with the poems?

- Read the opening and closing poems from this book – what impression do these poems give of the contents in-between, and do they suggest a sort of trajectory or narrative has taken place between the two points of departure and arrival?
- Next, look at the structure of these poetry collections. Do they break into distinct sections, have a form or theme that creates a structure, or is there some other form of structure at work in the ordering – i.e. chronological, narrative-based or thematic arc?
- Discuss the variety of approaches between you. Which work best? Do you find any parallels with your own poetry manuscripts?

Now, return to your own manuscripts and take some of this inspiration with you:

- Look at the poems in your manuscript; are you happy with the titles, or are some of them a bit too obvious or humdrum? Revisit them and come up with some alternatives that are more intriguing, better suited or would make you want to read on.
- What order is going to work best for you? Don't feel you have to pick something very strict or formal, with poems that are similar all grouped together. Or that you have to group poems on one theme (or on one kind of mood) all together, either – as this can also get quite predictable.

Themes can come and go, you can break up poems that are all around similar ideas or topics and come back to them later on, allowing dissimilar poems to sit next to each other and create interesting juxtapositions. If you want to be a bit more daring, you can even create moments where the reader is 'jolted' from one place to the next.

Think of it like building a good playlist or mix-tape – you may want to carefully orchestrate the moods, places and times a reader will move through, and sometimes you may want to take a sharp turn to somewhere altogether different. Play about with order and notice how this affects the feel and trajectory of the manuscript, and the various territories of mood, topic and ideas it will move through.

The Poem Order card game

This game (see overleaf) is intended as a bit of fun, but hopefully with a useful result. There is no right or wrong answer for this activity. Simply photocopy the table and cut out the different 'types' of poem so each is on a slip of paper or card of its own. Imagine these are your poems, and you're trying to order them for a pamphlet. Try them in a variety of different orders. Notice how different orders will create different effects.

A fun and flippant poem about forgetful relatives.	An angry poem about corrupt politicians/bankers.
The poignant poem about losing a loved one.	The experimental poem about moths around a lightbulb.
The parody poem of 'Do Not Go Gentle into That Good Night'.	The poem about being lost in wonder in a beautiful midsummer garden.
The mildly erotic poem.	The surreal poem about meeting Oscar Wilde in a lift in a department store.
The tender poem about a parent's old age.	The love poem set on an autumn beach in Wales.
The heartfelt poem about injustice and greed.	The humorous poem about being dumped by a lover on a wet Wednesday.

Finally, a quick note on this point about workshops, critique groups and friendly advice...

In order to ensure a good, healthy dynamic in any kind of workshop or group critique, always make sure the advice both given and received in these workshops is constructive, i.e. not just a case of saying 'I really like this' every time. Productive and valuable critique will be robust but will also identify with care what is and isn't working and offer some form of practical advice as to how you can remedy or develop the work.

Constructive critique should also always be sensitive – it should ask questions of a poet rather than make pronouncements on their work, and give space to explain, discuss or examine what is happening within a poem. It's good to have challenging advice but this should always be clearly coming from a place of positive critical concern and thoughtful engagement with the poem, and seek to offer technical resolutions to flaws or problems within a poem. It should never stray into personal critique, passive-aggression or the wholesale demolition of a poem without any positive investigation of solutions.

If you find the critique of a particular pairing or group isn't helping you, the best advice is always to move on. Seek advice that is challenging but useful, that is trustworthy and comes from a skilled source with constructive things to offer. Find the advice and feedback that will also offer you room to grow and not rest on your laurels too much. If you're seriously looking to develop your work, ensure that the critique and input comes from writers whose skills are at a stage a little further on from your own, so that your horizons are always being broadened and challenged. There's nothing wrong in outgrowing a workshop or feedback group if you find the advice is no longer providing enough positive and constructive grist to your creative mill.

CHAPTER TWENTY-THREE
How a Bathtub Can Change Your Life
(and six other loosely-connected thoughts about poetry)
by Rishi Dastidar

The following is a mostly true account of my journey through poetry so far. It doesn't have a straightforward argument or narrative; it's instead a series of thoughts or vignettes about poetry – performing it and writing it – and some of the overlap between writing copy for advertising, branding and design (my day job) and writing poems. Just think of this as an extended poem.

1: A bathtub can change your life

OK, not a bathtub as such but rather a poem about them. And I don't exaggerate when I say that the poem – and the book I found it in – changed my life.

The poem is called 'Bathtubs', and both it and the book, *Ashes for Breakfast*, are by a German poet called Durs Grünbein. Here's a little taste of the poem:

> What adorable objects bathtubs are, enamelled
> and sleek and altogether
> unapproachable with their
>
> heroic curves of wrought-iron
> old ladies still frisky
> after the menopause.

It was the spring of 2007, and I'd just come back from a weekend in Berlin and was looking for something to commemorate the trip. In those days there was still a Borders bookshop on Oxford Street, London's main shopping street, so I popped in there one Monday lunch time. Going up the escalator, my eye chanced upon this book. I picked it up, started flicking through it, and please don't laugh but honestly, it's as close to a religious moment I'm ever going to have in my life. I vividly remember thinking – *what is this stuff? Why don't the lines go all the way to the end of the page? Why has no one told me you could do this with words?*

I knew at that moment that I had found my thing – the thing that I wanted to write, that I will spend the rest of my days writing. Which was quite useful, as I had spent the previous 14 years knowing that I wanted to write and be a writer, but not having any real idea of what to write.

Pretty much the next day I signed up to do an introduction to poetry course at CityLit, a college in London – and that was it. I've been trying to be a poet ever since.

2: You sometimes have to stand on tables to get noticed

What no one tells you when you start trying to become a poet is that there isn't one single, obvious way of going about it. You end up trying a lot of things, some of which are, in retrospect, ludicrous.

Very early on, well before I was even remotely ready, I agreed to go and do an open mic session at a pub in Hoxton, a grittily fashionable part of East London.

(A side note: I know everyone says you should 'take every opportunity', especially if you don't know how to do something, 'just figure it out as you go'. But be warned – often the sole use of these experiments is to experience the burning pain of embarrassment, because apparently doing something badly is much more valuable when it comes to learning than if you do something well.)

Anyway, I didn't ask any questions about it – another mistake – I just turned up… to discover that the place was absolutely rammed… with people watching football.

Three people had turned up for the poetry. And there was no microphone.

Now what I should have done was turned tail and fled into the night. Instead, I stood on a table, then bellowed – and I really do mean bellowed, to the point at which I had no voice for the next few days – some very bad poems at those three bemused people.

This was in retrospect an early taste of one of the secrets of poetry that people don't tell you until later – often you have to win over your readers one by one.

I just didn't realise that that was literally going to be the case.

3: You start more poems than you ever finish

And that's okay. Poetry is a game of persistence. Often you have to wait for the poems to arrive – there's one in my book, *Ticker-tape*, called 'These things boys do', which took about a year, from the moment I thought of the idea for it, to it actually being finished. Speaking to some other poets, this apparently makes me a fast mover.

The point is that you have to hold your nerve, and trust your instinct that something will turn up. It normally does.

You have to wait on submissions too, hearing about whether you've had any joy in persuading a magazine to take your work. The only certainty here is that you will be rejected often, and have the pleasure of waiting a long time to find out.

And this is doubly frustrating because poetry is the only art where you can have a complete, finished piece in less than 30 minutes. It was said of Frank O'Hara that at parties you could challenge him to write a poem. He would then disappear to the bathroom for 20 minutes or so, to emerge triumphantly with a perfect, flawless poem.

An elegant party trick for sure, but as another of my heroes, Clive James, has said there is no greater pleasure than sitting down in a café with a coffee, knowing that even before you have finished your drink you could have written something that the world will be reading 500 years later.

So to continue to enjoy writing poems, you have to cultivate something I call 'patient impatience'. You have to be open to the image, the phrase, the conceit arriving at any moment, and yet you have to not feel or be panicked when nothing is coming, which can be – will be – quite often.

I'm not advocating being passive or doing nothing: you must always be reading, drafting, scribbling. But fallow periods, however long or short, are never just that – there is always something going on under the surface; it just might not seem like it.

4: It takes about 10 years to get good at doing poems

Here's another rule of thumb: it takes about 10 years on average for someone to be really ready to start publishing their poetry – the equivalent of Malcolm Gladwell's 10,000 hours of practice you need to get good at doing anything.

Now, considering the lack of financial rewards on offer, and then the slow process of getting noticed by magazine editors, publishers, radio people, booking agents – basically, you have to really, *really* want to write poems. Which means that most poets you meet are, how can I put this politely, *a little intense*.

Poetry is the branch of the entertainment industry that is closest to a religious vocation – a calling rather than a 9-5, regular office hours way of making a living.

When you get a chance, ply any poet with alcohol – and trust me, it won't take much – and ask them why? Why do you write this stuff when you could be crashing out popular novels, TV series, Hollywood screenplays? And eventually, after some faux modest huffing and puffing, you'll see the glint in the eye. The glint that says, 'I really like making patterns out of words on a page; arranging language so that it goes into the ears and the eyes and then captures a heart. Yes, all you other writers can have success, but you do not have what I have, which is a power to change the very atoms of someone's soul.'

I didn't say we were rational.

5: Constraints are liberating

You might have guessed by now that most poets are, in addition to everything else, masochists. We have to be, to do this slightly weird, semi-secret thing that we do. And then, on the basis of most contrary evidence, to expect the world to be interested in our outpourings.

And so here's one of the ways in which poetry and copywriting overlap – most poets love a tight brief, a constraint.

The thing I tell students – which always makes their faces fall – is: learn to write within the forms, within the rules, because when you break them later, you will do so with a style and a flourish you might not otherwise achieve.

And as in so many things, someone else said this better first, in this case Paul Muldoon: He said: 'Form is a straitjacket in the way that a straitjacket was a straitjacket for Houdini.'

6: The 17th draft may be a charm but probably isn't

My claim here is that there really is such a thing as over-drafting. You can worry at and rewrite a thing so much that you can effectively kill it, or at least the energy it needs to animate itself, to live in the ear of the reader and the listener. Or you forget the impulse that caused you to want to write the thing in the first place. It's a hard thing to spot, but you do have to learn to look out for it. What I'm trying to say is: yes, keep tinkering, keep tuning the words, for that is part of our craft – but part of our craft also has to be knowing when to stop and put down the pen. And I genuinely think that's something that's not said enough.

Honestly, the best writers are mostly lazy, and that's actually the secret of their success. Or am I just projecting here?

7: Copywriting is the unacknowledged patron of contemporary poetry

Genuinely, I can't imagine giving up my day job any time soon. Not just because I can't afford to – let me be candid with you here. No one ever lives off the money they earn from publishing poems, or even more rarely winning competitions or awards. Poetry is the ultimate 'slash' career – we are poets slash lecturers, poets slash teachers, poets slash civil servants and poets slash copywriters.

But also because I think the poetry does make me a better copywriter. Because it does give me something that feeds back into client work. A desire to take a few more risks maybe. A greater ability to weigh up words well perhaps. Bravery in choosing to use outlandish verbs, even. (By the way, using rare or unusual verbs is the quickest way to look like a genius in poetry, at least – this is advice to make the prose wallahs wince.)

And if you need convincing, let me tell you of some words in *Ogilvy on Advertising*, written by David Ogilvy, the founder of Ogilvy and Mather, still one of the world's largest advertising agencies. He quotes William Maynard as saying: 'Most good copywriters fall into two categories. Poets. And killers. Poets see an ad as an end. Killers as a means to an end.' And then, genius that he is, Ogilvy adds: 'If you are both killer and poet, you get rich.'

Well, it's something to aim for.

Rishi Dastidar's poetry has been published by the *Financial Times*, Tate Modern and the Southbank Centre and featured in the anthologies *Adventures in Form* (Penned in the Margins) and *Ten: The New Wave* (Bloodaxe). A fellow of The Complete Works, the Arts Council England funded programme for BAME poets, he is a consulting editor at *The Rialto* magazine, a member of the Malika's Poetry Kitchen collective, and serves as a chair for Spread The Word. His debut poetry collection, *Ticker-tape*, was published in 2017 by Nine Arches Press.

CHAPTER TWENTY-FOUR
How to Take the Publication Plunge

One of the questions I am most frequently asked by poets is *how do I know when I'm ready to get published?*

As a rough guide, you are ready once you have built up a good track record of publication in print and online magazines or journals, and you have some independent and external indication that your work is at publishable standard. A record of publication (as well as other useful achievements you can mention – like placements for prizes or competitions, live events, performances, online content or commissions) show that others like what you're doing and are keen to share it with their readerships and audiences, too. In addition, you should be at the stage where you have that wide enough portfolio of poems that you're happy are strong enough to go into a final manuscript, and the body of work surrounding them that has built up towards this point.

It's important to think about what you want to achieve and what's right at this stage for you (i.e. pamphlet or collection?). It's also about encouraging you to prize and respect your poetry, to value the time and energy that has gone into it, and urge you to research the many publishers that are out there, so that you can find the right fit for your poems, and a publisher you will be happy to work with.

You will no doubt feel trepidation, and you'll have some questions. So let's answer those now, shall we?

What kind of publishers are out there? Most poetry publishers fall into roughly three categories:

Major publishers
Most of these publishers are large and long-established independents, or imprints which are part of much larger media and publishing corporations.

They have large budgets, and the ability to promote and sell poetry books nationally and worldwide. You'll see a selection of their best-selling titles in every high-street book-retailer. They tend to publish well-known contemporary poets, plus your 'Classic Dead Poets' and general poetry anthologies.

These publishers rarely take on new poets for first collections, or only a very limited number each year. Some may have a policy of not accepting unsolicited manuscripts or have limited or no open submissions policy.

Large to medium-sized independent publishers

Most of these publishers may be relatively small businesses by comparison but are renowned and long-established, and often punch well above their weight in terms of the success of the poets they publish and the books they produce. There will be many familiar, well-known names on these publishers' lists.

These publishers will represent a range of new and established contemporary poets, and there is a greater chance of taking on new poets and debut collections with publishers of this kind of size. In general, these publishers will publish books, not pamphlets, and will seek a good, well-proven track record of publication from the poets they take on. A pamphlet and/or a reasonable amount of previous magazine publication are usually essential before submitting to these publishers.

Many of these publishers are partly supported by grants and arts funding. They are often more likely to take more risks but still need to see that the poet has an audience to sell to before they risk their money. These publishers may have submissions windows, but are generally open to submissions and unsolicited manuscripts.

Smaller independent presses

This category covers everything from handmade-pamphlet publishers of one or two new titles a year, right up to growing professional presses with busy lists and up to a dozen or so new books or pamphlets a year.

Small presses are independent and publish a wide and lively variety of books, pamphlets, magazines etc. They will often have open submissions, run competitions, or have an open reading window process for submissions. Smaller presses do have smaller trade reach and retail representation, and though they may lack the staffing and budgets of their larger counterparts, they do often make up for what they lack in size with their enthusiasm, their ability to spot talent, organise events and to support new voices.

They may also be more likely to take a risk on a poet who hasn't yet fully established a track record, or is at the earlier stages of development but shows plenty of promise and potential.

How do I find a good publisher?

It's really important to do your homework and research the range of publishers currently publishing poetry. Study the form of publishers and get a feel for their style, tastes and tendencies. Work out which presses you like, who you think you'd like to work with and whether your work 'fits' in a broad sense with their list.

As well as doing research online, please do buy some of the publisher's books or pamphlets if you can afford to do so and get a flavour of their output. I'm not simply saying this out of self-interest as a publisher: it will give you a better idea of what kind of things you can expect from each publisher in terms of style, quality and the type of poetry each seems to prefer. But also by spending your poetry pounds you are supporting (in your own a small but vital way) the same poetry economy you are hoping will ultimately support your own writing. Many independent poetry publishers are modest operations with only a few full-time members of staff, dependent on funding but also on their book-sales income to stay in business and survive and thrive to publish another day.

Support your local bookshop where you can, and remember that book borrowing (and requesting) helps to keep your local library afloat and demonstrates that real-life borrowers and readers still like to visit and use them.

The annual 'Free Verse' Poetry Book Fair in London is a good way to meet lots of poetry publishers all at once, and see their publications on display. And look out for the regional festivals and conferences where you might be able to find Q&As with publishers and editors, or showcases with presses and publishers. A number of festivals (such as Ledbury Poetry Festival) now also record or film their events, so it's worth checking out their websites to see if you can catch up later with publisher showcases or Q&As which may be useful in giving you an insight into a publisher's tastes and ideas of what they're looking for. Also, editors quite often give online interviews, so why not search them out and see what the editors themselves have to say about what they look for in a poetry manuscript, and the kind of work they are looking to publish.

One small plea, however: *please* do not go to events, festivals or conferences armed with copies of your manuscript (or, with an escalator pitch prepared and a CV) and then attempt to foist these onto every publisher you meet. Whilst I and most of my fellow editors are always happy to talk about submissions, or how best to get your work in front of us, and the kind of thing we're looking for, we really don't want to have a manuscript forced on us along with the expectation of feedback and a further correspondence (the business card, the promotional flyer, the offer of travelling to come and have a meeting with us...). It's all a bit too soon, and it really isn't a good way to go about submitting your work.

How do I get a submission together?

Depending on the publisher, you'll be asked to either send in hard copy or submit your manuscript digitally via email or a submissions management app like Submittable. Either way, you should check their guidelines for specific preferences.

If not specified, present the poems as follows:

- In a regular plain font, such as Times New Roman, Arial, Garamond or Palatino Linotype.
- 12pt font size in black.
- On plain white A4 paper.
- No more than one poem to a page.
- If submitting to a magazine, add a footer to the bottom of each page with your name, email and / or address in case the covering letter and poems go adrift. For poetry manuscripts, you could simply add your name and title of the manuscript to the footer.

You will also need a covering letter or email. This should ideally be one page or side of A4 and contain:

- The editor's name(s).
- Your address and email.
- A basic introductory paragraph saying what you are submitting and giving a brief outline of your poetry.
- A short biographical note ideally not more than 100-150 words, including details of your publishing track record.
- If posting them, a note as to whether you require the poems returning (and include a stamped addressed envelope for this purpose) or recycling.
- Finally, thank the editors for their time in considering your work. Sign off.

If you are unsure about the procedure or form of the submission in any way, it is always better to email and ask before submitting your work. Make sure first that your query isn't already covered in the guidelines or in the advice on their website.

Finally, send it off. Good luck!

CHAPTER TWENTY-FIVE
On Success

'All you need to know about literary prizes is
Shakespeare never won one.' – Anon

For many of us, 'success' means the visible success of prizes, publications and public reputation. These rewards are precious and encouraging, and I'll discuss them below: but the kind of success we should pursue most actively is rather different.

Magazines and Journals

Poetry journals are the main forum for new poets to get exposure and recognition. They will typically publish one or two of your poems at a time, alongside a wide variety of other work. Visit the Poetry Library's website for a list of the current journals, and look at their websites for an idea of their style. UK journals almost never pay for work, and will often keep you waiting for many months to let you know if they want your poems. Nonetheless, do not submit the same poem to two journals at once. I've said a good deal about this in Chapter Seventeen.

Many people send to smaller journals or competitions 'to begin with' and tell themselves that they will work up to the bigger ones. This is particularly true of women, as research and personal experience has shown time and again – the female poet is particularly prone to being consumed by under-confidence. Life is short, dear reader. You may never feel worthy of the journals you most admire. Trust me, as a sometime judge and editor: very many of the people who do send work to *Poetry Review* are entirely unhindered by self-doubt. If you are in any doubt as to your skill, you are already in a minority whose work is more likely to be worth reading. Many fine poets sit wringing their hands over the sixtieth draft of a poem, imagining that all the work sent to *The Rialto* or *Magma* is of Nobel Prize quality. There is nothing to be gained by staring at it any longer. Put a stamp on it or stick it in an email, send it off and think no more of it for six months. It gets easier, I promise.

A journal which asks for a maximum of six poems does not mean 'send us six poems'. If you send only three, then you can send to twice as many journals. Choose your own strategy for the number of poems you send. As with competitions, send the work you are most proud of to the journals you most admire, and let the editors decide if they want to publish you.

Competitions

Poetry competitions are plentiful. For the winners they offer visible success, validation by a notable judge and perhaps some prize money. The larger ones may have a press release announcing winners, and will spread the word on social media. Competitions also have an advantage over journals, in that they usually announce results on a fixed date. If you are unlucky, at least you know that your work is definitely free to send off to other competitions or journals. By all means enter the big, prestigious competitions – the National Poetry Competition in the UK attracts around 13,000 entries each year – and let no-one dissuade you. Too often capable poets say they are 'not ready' for the big competitions, but a good poem doesn't come with a CV saying how long the poet has been writing; it will catch the judge's eye anyway, so send it off.

Do, however, consider smaller competitions like the Manchester Cathedral Poetry Prize or the Buzzwords prize, which supports a thriving poetry community. A brand new competition or one with a special remit such as ecology will have fewer entries, so your chance of success is greater. The Poetry Library has an email newsletter and a good section on competitions on their website. Poetry journals usually carry adverts for competitions, and social media is also a good source. If you've never heard of the judge or the organisation, and the prize is negligible, then ask yourself whether there is any real benefit in winning.

As with journals, look at the submission guidelines. If the competition specifies a forty-line limit that doesn't mean that you have to write forty lines. The judge will probably weep with relief at the sight of a poem which is ten or twenty lines long. It does, however, mean that anything more than forty lines is ineligible. The judge will not make an exception for your brilliant forty-two-line masterpiece; they will simply set it aside. Don't try to second-guess the judge, or send poems which you think are like their own. Whenever I judge a competition I find a suspicious number of poems about canals (I live on a boat, but am not likely to rate a bad poem any higher because it has a boat in it). A colleague who writes rather surreal, magical imagery finds a predominance of mermaids and hummingbirds in the work submitted to her. It's a little insulting to imagine that we can only enjoy work like our own. Choose a competition with a judge whose work you admire, send off your best work and trust them to value it on its own terms.

Most competitions have an entrance fee, and some are very expensive to enter. The Manchester Poetry Prize, the Poetry Business pamphlet prize and some others charge a substantial fee. Why? Because the prize money has to come from somewhere. Because the judges have to be paid for their time, especially if they are reading pamphlet-length submissions. Because the administration and marketing of a big competition takes resources. Because poetry competitions are almost always fund-raisers for the organisation running them – in many cases, the only source of income. If the fee is too much then don't enter the competition, but don't gripe about paying it. Poetry organisations are almost always run by hard-pressed volunteers, or writers who are trying to make the thing pay its own costs. If you enter a competition and don't win, then you and hundreds of others are at least paying something in to the poetry ecology that you're a part of. You enable talented writers to get a leg-up. Their success does not diminish yours; be happy for them and keep writing.

Publication

The generally accepted 'career path' for poets is this: you get a few poems published in reputable journals. You gather these and others into a short collection and submit it to a pamphlet publisher like Happenstance or the Poetry Business. You get a pamphlet published, and then you submit a full manuscript to a reputable publisher like Bloodaxe, Nine Arches (ahem) or Seren. The pamphlet stage is not essential, but it does help to gather an audience who will be on your side when a full-length collection comes out.

If you think you are ready to submit a full-length manuscript, then go ahead. Check out the publisher you are interested in, find out if they are accepting work and if so, in what format, and send it. A publisher will want a pool of strong poems, from which to choose around 40-50 for a full collection. As a broad rule of thumb, if you've been writing poetry for less than five years you are not likely to get a collection published by a recognised publisher. I say this not to discourage you but because it's simply true. They will want to know that many of your poems have been published in journals, which indicates that you're serious about your work and that there might already be a readership for it.

Not many poetry publishers in the UK will pay an advance. If your work is accepted then there may be a wait of a year or two before publication, and you'll be paid a share of the sales in royalties. The UK sales figures for poetry do not gladden the heart. At least we poets can give ourselves literary airs and graces, telling novelists and non-fiction writers that we practice our art for art's sake. The fact that we have to, because nobody pays us to practice it, is neither here nor there.

A word on self-publishing, and it is a harsh word. People often kid themselves that self-publishing is just as good as mainstream publishing now. It simply is not. For a pamphlet it may well suffice: the print run will be small, you have full control of your first work in print, and you can print to a high quality. For a full-length collection, however, self-publishing is usually counter-productive in terms of reputation and output. Ask yourself very truthfully why you want a book out: is it just for the pleasure of having a book with your name on it? Then go ahead. Self-publish and be damned. It will give you real pleasure, and you can sell it at readings and give it to friends. Admit, though, that you will not edit, design or market it as well as a publishing house whose business is to do these three things, which has built contacts and whose income depends on the quality of their output. Nor will most publishers accept the work later, which you have already published. A publishing house, in fact, won't put out work which falls below its usual standard. It's because of that ruthless eye that we trust publishers as arbiters of good work, and go to them when we're looking for it.

It is true that some great books have been self-published, but the fact is that most self-published authors take this route precisely because they can't face the difficult and painful process of being edited by someone who will push them to make their work better. It would be lovely if we could gain a reputation with no cost to our ego, but in poetry as in almost any other walk of life, that seldom happens. If you want to take part in the wider poetry culture and simply get better at writing, then you must open your work to criticism at the writing stage (through local writing groups or online forums) at the editing stage (through the input of a professional publisher whose choices may differ from yours) and at the post-publication stage (from reviewers who may miss the point or simply dislike your work). In every case where I've been handed a self-published book, the quality of the work is disappointing.

We all want validation and praise, but surely in poetry real success is something else. Don't get me wrong: I have won competitions, been published in journals, and my poetry collections have sold relatively well. That's all very nice indeed, and gives me a sense of validation for which I am very grateful. We can't all be like Emily Dickinson, writing privately for a lifetime and only finding acclaim after death. It *is* satisfying to know that your peers value your work enough to give you a gong or put you in print. It *is* an ego-boost to think that your words are reaching an audience, or get a message from a stranger saying that your poem has moved them. If a national newspaper or a commissioning editor wants your work to appear under their banner, then you will certainly get a rosy glow of pleasure.

If fame and fortune are what you're after, then you might perhaps have made a mistake in choosing poetry as an art form. Poetry, like other art forms, is one way to try and make sense of our lives. It is a conversation and constant working out of what to do next, how to tackle difficult subjects, how to deal with the circumstance and incident of life. You will never know how to do it, completely. You will never have an epiphany where you feel that your poetry education is over, and you can now write with perfect confidence in your own voice and values. Just as you get a sure foothold on the major names of contemporary poetry, some bright new star will arrive to unsettle you and make you question everything. You will never have read all the classics. There will always be someone who is better read than you, or who knows more about the techniques and tools of poetry than you do. There may occasionally be someone who, with slightly less talent than you, gets published in *The Journal of Very Cool New Poetry* because they are sleeping with the editor.

If you aspire to publication, prizes and immortality, that's all well and good but keep your focus on making work. Your private success is the one that will sustain you: the continuing effort to write your own poetry as well as you can, to explore your own experience, to keep developing as an artist. Your project as a poet is to learn, to practise and to accept that every scrumpled draft is another step towards a poem you can be really pleased with. Sharing your work with a wider community is a further step. It gives you a chance to hear praise or useful feedback, and to contribute the same to the creative ecology of which you are a part.

Putting those worldly prizes and validations out of your head when you write, so that you have complete creative freedom, is not an entirely saintly approach. As it happens, it's also the best way to attain those rewards.

We called this book *How to Be a Poet,* not *How to Write Poetry.* Being a poet is not a mystical vocation, but there is more to it than just writing poetry and publishing it. It is a practice of looking closely at the world, of absorbing others' writing and distilling your own thoughts into words. 'Being a poet' is not about pure introspection. It's an active way of relating to your environment, your community and yourself. It offers you a constant refreshment of perspective, and a life of generous interaction with other writers. Perhaps poems are only the symptom of this outlook. In the final analysis, not all poetry is equal: but the process of writing it, and of exploring one's life by doing so, is equally valuable for each writer.

CHAPTER TWENTY-SIX
How to Stand Out in the Submissions Pile

I'm regularly asked what exactly it is I am looking for in a submission, and what kind of things will make a submission stand out from the crowd in any submissions pile. It's a good question, but often I do wonder if the enquirer is hoping I may be able to let a trade secret slip – give them the golden clue or magic ingredient that, if simply blended with their poems or sprinkled like pixie dust over a manuscript, will help to make a submission an irresistible prospect to a publisher.

It's worth saying that 99% of what I love in any manuscript I have accepted for publication is already present in the original submission. The final 1% may be attributed to the editing and polishing we do together, a poem or two we may add or how we tweak the order of poems and structure overall of a collection, but I have to feel that the manuscript already has all the right ingredients *before* I take it on.

Bear in mind also that my mind will be pretty much made up within the first ten pages of a submission. You have ten chances to grab my attention – if these first poems are all of a very similar standard or rather disappointing, I will be very close to having made my conclusions about the submission.

I recently calculated that in an average year I read and consider somewhere in the region of 9,000 individual poems as part of submissions for *Under the Radar* magazine, Nine Arches Press and the Primers scheme combined. This doesn't include any I may read also if I'm judging poems for competitions, as I sometimes do, and the many poems I will also read for pleasure or leisure in my spare, non-editing, reading time.

The question is, how does one assess this volume of poetry, and what do we learn from reading so much of it? For me, there are three levels at which I would categorise the submissions I receive and consider:

- **Level One**

At a rough estimate, from any average sample of 100 manuscripts submitted, about **50%** of those submissions will be an instant and very obvious No and will be quickly declined. In quite a few instances, I will know my decision within the first few poems, and will have made my mind up for sure within the first dozen poems in almost every case.

There will be a variety of reasons for this submission being rejected so quickly, which will include some or all of the following:

Poetry at a very early stage of development. That's not to say these poets will never be published or should stop, but rather that it's far too early to say. They haven't yet read or written enough poetry and out of the twenty poems I may see in their manuscript, they may have only so far written another thirty or forty poems in total. There isn't yet evidence of the skills, experiences and ideas to make the poems good enough for publication.

Poetry that predominantly tells and very rarely shows. On occasion, these poems may seem to be barely disguised, badly-written prose arranged into a poem shape. The poems will feel instructional or involve a series of blank or bald statements that lack depth (i.e. one-dimensional poems on current affairs) or any opportunity for the reader to bring their imagination to bear and be actively involved within the poems in any way.

Poetry that uses archaic language or poetry which is written in bad pastiche or parody of a classic poet or classical work. Epic poems about the faerie kingdom, mystical dolphins or journeys through myth that rework them in modern or clunky rhymed narratives. The poet has clear delight in language and form but has not read any contemporary (or even modern, twentieth-century) poetry, and is unlikely to be familiar with my list or what I tend to publish.

Poetry at a very basic skill level. This may be what we might term 'doggerel'. Often humorous, preachy or very earnest. Sometimes obviously and heavily rhymed, often unexpurgated and unedited. The work feels raw, unworked and rarely redrafted. It lacks evidence of structure, form, craft or technique. It's clear that the poet in question has not read much, if any, poetry – contemporary or otherwise.

Poorly-crafted poetry for children or young adults. The poet does not fully understand, respect or engage with their intended audience. All too often written in the mistaken belief that children's literature is somehow 'easier' to write and just needs to be nonsensical and rhyming to appeal.

Poetry written to vent an opinion or grievance. These poems may be rants, or have a particular agenda. This may include offensive or problematic poems that use racist, sexist, ableist, or classist language, or which draw heavily on stereotypes. Sometimes this may also include poems which handle sensitive topics or themes badly, leaving the poems unclear and open to interpretation. Or where the poet has been careless, insensitive and thoughtless as to how others will experience their words.

• **Level Two**

At the next stage of my considerations, I will see a further **40%** of submissions which sit solidly in the middle ground, demonstrating varying degrees of promise which isn't yet quite fully developed. These submissions are still likely to be declined, but far less quickly.

These submissions demonstrate that the writer clearly has potential and skill as a writer, even if they are at a very early stage or do not yet know enough about their practice as a poet to make the most of it yet.

Within this second group is a sliding scale from *almost* awful, to *almost* rather very good. There's promise here and it's clearly a step up from the previous group, even if some similar mistakes are still evident on occasion. Predominantly, these are often poets that still need to read more widely, challenge themselves and move out of their comfort zones as writers.

It may also be the case that some of the most talented writers in the upper regions of this category are nearly there, but the manuscript they've sent doesn't quite float my boat. Or, they very simply need a publisher who isn't me – a press where their work will be better situated. For instance, I will sometimes read work of merit that is well-produced and carefully crafted, but where I feel that it's not quite the kind of work I'm either best equipped to edit, or that it may not quite suit my list (I try to keep a very broad list, but there will always be work I can see the potential in but isn't quite what I'm interested in or seek to publish). It may even be the case that it's a bit too similar to the work of poets I already have on my list, and wouldn't necessarily want 'more of the same'. In these instances, I tend to try and point the poet towards the right publisher – it's always tremendously heartening when collections are then picked up as a result, and later published.

More generally, poetry submissions at this stage may include some or all of the following flaws or common faults at work:

Cardboard cut-outs. This is the poetry of one-dimensional engagement. For example, these might be nature poems that describe nature or encounters, such as a hawk circling over a moor, but without a greater sense that the experience has been as thoroughly explored as it could be, or that there are other deeper dimensions to the poem beyond passive observance. It's possible to write a good poem about this subject, but the best ones will go beyond the hawk, and are rarely *just* a poem about a hawk. The poem should take me elsewhere – touch or hint at (for instance) matters of sex or mortality, or why leaving somewhere or someone you love is difficult. A good poem always changes something in the reader, rather than simply reinforcing their existing knowledge: *Oh look, a rare bird of prey. I've seen one, you know...* Some ekphrastic or heavily-themed poetry can be culpable of this if the poems are not as fully developed as they should be – especially where the poem is not venturing beyond describing the art or theme it engages with. This kind of poetry will fail to take that extra vital step: it will never be charged with the vital lightning bolt that strikes and illuminates, taking us beyond the flat plane of merely describing things well.

Poetry as emotional tourism. I read examples of these poems far too often, unfortunately. This is the kind of poem that tends to go along the lines of: *'oh I saw a poor old beggar / homeless person / child / refugee etc.., and I gave them some money / food / clothes and it was all terribly humbling and I looked into their eyes and saw great spiritual wisdom / humble forgiveness etc. / And came away from it all feeling terribly enlightened'*. This sort of poem feels cheap and exposes a certain kind of privilege at work. If you want to write about other people's experience of being poor or underprivileged it's really vital you first consider the position of privilege you are writing from. See Chapter Fifteen for Jo's take on how to avoid this and write successful political and polemical poems.

The poetry collection as postcard. *I went to Italy last year. It was hot and sunny. I've written a whole book about my travels in Tuscany...* Whilst we're glad you had a lovely holiday or gap year, it doesn't tend to make for the most thrilling poetry, and comes across as poetry as tourism or guidebook – again lacking that deeper engagement, we readers become merely sightseers into an experience. There are ways to make this work, but you need to have approaches and slants to the work that simply goes beyond a surface-level visitor's exploration of somewhere sunny or historic.

Poetry that relies on the reversal of syntax. *'Cold, I felt, that afternoon'*. A little red light flashes and the buzzer goes off on my poetry scanner when one of these tries to get through the security barriers…

Poetry that engages with 'the big themes' badly. These poems attempt to meet the big themes (the spiritual, love, war, death) entirely head-on, straight-faced, and with a heavy hand. This poetry lacks subtlety and the careful circumnavigation required to really get to the heart of matters with precision. Don't forget Emily Dickinson's advice to 'Tell the truth, but tell it slant'. The poet here is yet to take the quantum leap in their practice where they move from meeting everything at face value to the point where they can use tactful workaround routes and diversions to bring the truth of things much more clearly into focus.

Poetry that engages with postmodern or experimental practices, but not very skilfully. Sometimes there is a misunderstanding that you can get away with anything simply because you are writing experimental poetry. The best experimental work pushes at boundaries and presents truly surprising ideas and approaches, the worst will feel derivative and no doubt something an editor has seen many times before.

Also,

weird   poem
              L A Y O U T S
do   not   mean
    the   poem   is
        A C TU A LL Y   any   good

Poetry that uses and reuses the same format, structure or style in every poem. Sometimes a poet will have developed a particular formula for making a poem. That might be something that feels reliable and comfortable to them, but it does result in the poems all feeling a little monotonous by the time I am past the first dozen or so and have spotted the formula at work. It might be a structural formula such as:

Object + Occurrence = Revelation

or far too many of these kind of regular compounds:

Adjective + Noun + Verb
(i.e. frosted trees leaning, weary travellers wandering, ancient bridges shadowing...)

If you're using a repetitive formula to help to build almost every poem you write, you do need to consider disrupting your usual patterns. Be aware also of the too-neat ending, or a tendency for every poem to end or begin in the same way.

Poetry manuscripts in which the first few poems are good but the rest of the manuscript either repeats the ideas without developing them further, or circles around ideas without going anywhere. Reading the whole manuscript, I'll wonder what I can remember from it, if anything, and if there's a sense of anything having changed in my reading from beginning to end.

• Level Three

Finally, we come to the top **10%** and the very best submissions I will see in a submissions window. Here you will find the work that is there – or very nearly there. This is poetry that will excite and delight me, for one or more of the various factors:

The work is surprising. Things don't quite happen in the poems as you expect. I find this extremely attractive and hard to resist. I want to read on, I am drawn in and involved.

The writing is clear and precise. There is no obfuscation for its own sake, though there will be lines that are at once adventurous and apparent.

And that's not to say this work is simplistic, plain or merely clear. It can still be complex and challenging for all its clarity – the perfect combination. This is work that doesn't just state the obvious. Work and effort from the reader is an integral part of it. It feels like we're hand in hand with the poems, discovering them for ourselves.

This is work that is adventurous. It might be quietly so, this isn't about adventure for its own sake, but rather a sense of challenge and risk as something integral to the work. It might be exploring topics or themes that are different or new, or familiar ones in a new way or via a different approach. It may be adventurous in the forms the poems take, or the way they play around with language, or subvert and toy with the expectations of the reader.

The collection may or may not be heavily-themed or written around one concept, but there will always be a thread of something, however subtle, that makes the poems hang together as a cohesive whole.

I get a powerful sense of where the poet is coming from, and what they have to say, and I feel I could sum up the collection pithily but not reductively in a sentence or two – and still feel there will be things to discover afresh on further readings. There may be a pervading and powerful sense of joy, discovery or loss in these poems, or they may allow a narrative of sorts to unfold informally between the poems as much as within them. I feel drawn in as a reader – keen to spend more time in the company of these poems.

Uniqueness of voice is also vital for me as an editor at this stage. What stands out above the clamour? The very best submissions will leave me with an almost eerie sense of presence from the strength of voice in the work – it will feel as if the writer is speaking, clearly and presently to me.

And the very top submissions within this top ten percent? This is the elusive gold dust we have been searching for – the real poetry treasure. These three or four submissions will contain the kind of poems that will keep me up at night, trouble me (in all the good and right ways), the poems that I will wake up to, their lines and ideas and images still tugging insistently at my sleeves. When I return to a manuscript like this, I know already, instinctively, that I will want to share these poems with readers too.

I share these rough conclusions from my submissions pile with an advisory pinch of salt: bear in mind that these ratios and rough estimations are based on my experiences of submissions of manuscripts, and that these margins will change if I am considering a competition or magazine submissions. And this is of course my own approach as an editor. You'll find many other editors would have plenty of criteria to add to this, and some points they may entirely disagree with. Just because something doesn't work for me, doesn't mean another editor won't be delighted, enamoured and enraptured by your poems. Keep going.

CHAPTER TWENTY-SEVEN
On Confidence

'The worst enemy to creativity is self-doubt.' – Sylvia Plath

Confidence is vital if you are to get anywhere with your writing, but one can have too much of a good thing. Some poets, entirely free of self-doubt, feel that they have been cheated of the renown to which they are entitled. Others, consumed by self-doubt, have a folder full of world-class poems which they never feel able to share.

Both the excess and the lack of confidence will stop you reaching your full potential. Over confidence, for instance, makes us impervious to feedback. If ten people tell you that a line needs changing, it probably does. Equally, if you approach a well-known publisher with a manuscript, having never read a journal or shared your work publicly before, you will likely be rejected. Don't be too wounded in either case. Negative feedback is more useful than praise. Take it as humbly as you can.

Also over-confident is the white poet who suspects that other people get published because they are black/ female/ transgender/ gay/ traumatised/ disabled or simply pretty, whilst their own work is neglected because it is not so 'exotic'. We have a long way to go before being white, educated, heterosexual or male is even a neutral state, let alone a disadvantage. The playing field is not yet level. Concentrate on your own work, and if it's good enough it will be heard.

If a surfeit of confidence gets in the way of seeing one's writing clearly, it can at least be useful in terms of persistence. Perhaps more dangerous to creative success is a lack of confidence; and in this area there is certainly a gender imbalance. For instance, in a recent survey for a report on diversity in British poetry most women ticked the box marked 'aim to achieve' whereas most men ticked 'expect to achieve'[2]. Not all men. Not all women. There are over-confident women and under-confident men, of course: but the pattern exists.

In my 52 project, an online community of over 600 poets, I lost count of the women who posted a poem of breath-taking quality and simply refused to believe any of the good feedback they received, seizing with a kind of hunger on anything negative. I have mentored women whose work is extraordinary, but who never send it to the journals they admire. They tell themselves that *The Rialto* or *Poetry Review* are not for the likes of them. They sign up to 'Beginning in Poetry' courses even when they have written for twenty years. They self-publish, assuming that established publishers would not be interested in their work without even trying. They don't enter poetry competitions, convinced that every other competitor is far above them. In short, they value their own skills too lightly and other people's too highly.

To such self-effacing writers, regardless of gender, we say: try not to put obstacles in your own way. Push yourself as hard as you can to get the things you actually want. All poets should try to get a sense of their worth – for good or bad. Learn it by mixing with other poets, by reading and by submitting your work to scrutiny by your peers in a writing group. Be ready to hear criticism, and to act on it. When you're sure a poem is as good as it can be, then own it and if reputation matters to you, then send it out in the world for others to enjoy. You are a part of the poetry ecology. You have a right to contribute, and a sort of duty to help others in their own learning. Your work will always be improving. You're entitled to take part, and you're entitled to all the support and feedback other poets can offer. Others may limit you, but don't limit yourself.

2.   Dr Nathalie Teitler, quoted from https://twitter.com/Natteitler/status/924235768834510848 in reference to The Complete Works survey as part of *Freed Verse: Diversity in British Poetry 2005-2017* report (28 Oct. 2017).

CHAPTER TWENTY-EIGHT
How to Build a Track Record
(and what editors are *really* looking for)

I began my previous chapter by talking about the question people frequently ask me – *what are you looking for in a poetry manuscript?* – and I'd like to return to this for a moment.

The answer I usually give is that there are three particular criteria I look for. But this will also be tempered by a disclaimer: I can't tell you what 'kind' of poetry manuscript I want to publish as I only know that when I find it. I can only tell you the commonalities and qualities I find alike in the kind of poetry I enjoy and accept and publish, those in the top few percent of every submissions pile.

Technical Quality

I'm looking for poetry that is written to a high standard. This is poetry that demonstrates care and craft in its construction, and which is absolutely deliberate in its making.

Like a well-made outfit, this kind of poetry isn't flash. The hard graft of its making, the stitching together and the seams are evidently part of structure but not visible on the surface. It appears effortless whilst also, clearly, much effort went into making it appear *just so*.

Creative Integrity

I am seeking poetry that is original and bold and which makes an unshakeable imaginative connection with its reader. For this to be the case, it has to also be poetry that is wholly itself. The poet does not write with anyone else's' borrowed cloak slung over their shoulders, and does not try to imitate the style of other contemporary poets. They trust their own voice to be strong enough to carry their work, even if that voice is at times trying various modes of delivery or inhabiting a multiplicity of characters or approaches. Something will still clearly anchor that voice; an inimitable and quietly-confident style which underpins the entire structure of their poetry.

The images, similes and metaphors will demonstrate that the poet is taking leaps and risks, and will come alive for the reader in a way that makes them feel implicated, involved and appreciated. These poets have put a great deal of craft and care into the form and structure of their poems and are deliberate in their choices of how the poem lives on the page. Nothing is incidental or left to chance. These poems are so good, you'll wish you'd have written them.

I believe that it is essential that a poem does three things:
- Makes a connection with its reader
- Changes something from the beginning to the end
- Speaks its own truth

Practical Considerations

Can I work with this writer, am I the right kind of editor for them, can we make this book work, who will buy this book and does this poet have an audience or the potential for an audience? This is the business part of the deal – and it is all about the head over heart.

It isn't simply a financial decision (though as a publicly-funded organisation, or as a limited company, the editor has a responsibility of some form to make their investment of time, money and resources back). I want a poet to succeed to the very best of their potential, and they can only do this if the writing is at the right stage and if there is already some established awareness of their work. I need to know that an investment of care and attention and resources will be rewarding for us both, and that I'm the right kind of publisher for the poet in question.

It is at this stage that demonstrating a track record is vital. Most publishers are highly unlikely to take on a collection or pamphlet by a poet that has no or very limited evidence of publication track record or audience.

With this in mind, let's take a slightly more detailed look at that final point, and what we really mean by it:

Why do you need a track record?

A track record tells the publisher that you have already done some of the work to establish your name as a poet and are keen to work to promote yourself and your poems. It also gives an indication of the quality of your work – that other editors also think it is worth publishing and potentially putting their money and energy and time behind your poems.

What is a track record?

By a track record of publication, we're not suggestion some kind of *Catch 22*-esque situation whereby in order to get a book published, you need already to have a book published. Rather, what we mean by this is that your poetry should have already received some publication in poetry magazines and journals. If you want to get a full collection of poems published it can be helpful if you have already published a pamphlet, but this is not essential.

It also useful to know about:

- Magazines, anthologies or other publications (print or online) where your poems have previously been published.
- Any prizes or competitions you've won, or been shortlisted, commended or longlisted for.
- Any projects or commissions you've been involved with as a poet.
- Any schemes or writer development programmes you've been part of.
- If you perform your work, perhaps mention events, open mics or festivals you have performed at.
- Any other poetry activities you might be involved with, even simply that you've been part of a Stanza group, or you have a regular blog that you write.

The most useful way to include this information is in the short biography you include with your covering letter. We don't expect a CV with a submission, but we do need to know that if we publish your work, not only will you have an audience of some form keen to see these poems, and hopefully buy your book, but also to see that the wider poetry community has perhaps spotted you also.

It is also important for an editor to feel they can work with a poet, and vice-versa. Make sure you approach a publisher you feel you can work with, whose books you like, and whose ethos fits with yours.

If a poet doesn't perform their poetry live, it's useful to know others ways in which their work is finding audiences – i.e. online, through other publications or film, social media, blogs or awards, which can often have equal (and sometimes greater weight) than live readings or public events.

Difficult Manuscripts

Remember that there is nothing stopping you seeking publication for a manuscript if you don't yet have much by way of track record, or if your manuscript is a little out of the ordinary (perhaps because it is an experimental, avant-garde, unusual or very specific kind of publication). However, it would be advisable to target it towards the right kind of publisher, one more willing to take a risk on a very new poet, or who specifically has an interest in your type of poetry.

Bear in mind that a limited track record *will* narrow your chances with potential publishers – it might be worth thinking of creative ways to get around this, like developing a bigger online profile for your poetry, or thinking of other ways your poems could get out there (like films, audio or podcasts).

Also, the following types of publication may have very specific limitations to their wider appeal and, in an already niche market, may face challenges in finding a suitable publisher:

Illustrated books or poetry with accompanying art or photography. The cost of reproducing high-quality colour images will be a deterrent for many publishers. Poetry is not (as you may have gathered) a publishing sector awash with money, and quite a lot of publishers have small print budgets for mainly mono-printed all-text collections. An equally expensive retail price to reflect print costs also means a potentially reduced sales reach and audience for such titles, making them less appealing. It would be advised that you seek a publisher who has previously published similar books, or specialises in them.

Children's Poetry. Children's and Young Adult publishing is a specialist area, and it is really worth doing research to understand the market before engaging in costly work on a manuscript that may not be suitable. It's advisable you find a publisher who already or specifically publishes this kind of poetry, and knows how to market it and seek audiences for it successfully.

Commission or Project-specific poetry. Certainly not *all* but *some* poetry manuscripts that result from residencies or commissions may be limited by how specific they are and what kind of audience they may expect beyond the immediate and initial one as part of project. It may be more worthwhile and expedient to publish or self-publish a small number as a special limited-edition or giveaway as part of the project or commission itself, or to see if a small press may like to partner on it.

Collaborations. These may share some similar difficulties as the project-based proposals as above. There may also be a sense that some parts of a collaborative manuscript are more successful than others, which may be difficult to remedy.

Publishing, and Not Publishing

Ultimately, you may also want to consider if publication through the traditional route is the right option for a particular group of poems, especially if you're finding it hard to place them with a publisher.

If this is the case, your options might be to:

- Accept that maybe publishing isn't right at this stage. Not everything you write will find a publisher, or perhaps *should* be published.
- Redraft or keep working on your poems. Or put them away and start writing something new. If you simply enjoy writing poems, no-one is stopping you. Does it really matter if they're not traditionally published?
- Examine the poems and seek professional advice or feedback on whether they are of publishable standard. Work to develop your skills as a poet. Find pleasure and enjoyment in the challenges of the craft, and don't worry too much about setting targets around publication.
- Find alternative ways to publish. Could you crowdfund this? We've previously mentioned film, audio and podcast outlets for poems, but you could also consider collaborating with artists or musicians and finding other outlets for your work that put your writing to good use?
- Jo does have a more draconian view of self-publishing than me, though I do broadly agree with her points on this matter. However, there are specific circumstances in which it might be a good option for some poets. If it's for a very specific purpose, project or audience, or if you simply want something to give to friends and family, your poems may fare better as a self-published eBook, pamphlet or book. Using a reputable print-on-demand service like Lulu.com, or a local printer who won't charge you a fortune to print a handful of pamphlets (and may even be able to help design it with you) may be a better route. Bear in mind the limitations of this option.

CHAPTER TWENTY-NINE
On Money

Money and poetry are seldom found in the same place. Nevertheless, it is possible to make a living as a poet. Note, I don't say 'by writing poetry'. Hardly anyone in contemporary Britain does that, including the greatest names you can think of. The best known poets are also lecturers, broadcasters, well-practised performers or have a hand in big poetry projects which pay them a retainer. There is however a small class of working poets who earn money through a mixed portfolio of poetry-related work. That work may include book sales, stage appearances, work in schools, writing to commission and residencies. Many of these people have a part-time job elsewhere, to give them a measure of security.

If you want to be one of those people, you may wonder how to get a foot on the ladder. There are a thousand answers. Many of them depend on taking unpaid work which isn't an option for all. Volunteering at a literary festival is a great way to get a feel for the kind of events, workshops and readings that attract a paying audience. Running an open mic night or monthly writing club is a thankless task, but will introduce you to many poets, including headliners, and establish your name as a poetry activist. Keep building your own work: write poetry, read good poetry and be ready for opportunities.

Above all, make opportunities for paid work. How do you get to be a writer in residence? Often by simply asking. Is there a local stately home or visitor attraction, a museum, a famous writer's house, a country park or theatre you'd like to work with? Call them up and explain what you'd like to do. 'My name is Bentley Crudsworth and I work in poetry. I love your display of historic coproliths and would like to be a writer in residence at your museum. I would want to come in to the museum for five days in the next three months, talk to your staff about their favourite exhibits, and write six poems for display alongside the objects or on your website. We could do a press release to say that I'll be there on the following dates, one of which will be during Open Heritage Week'. Quote a fee based on the number of days, and a daily rate you think is fair. This will vary according to your experience, your willingness to do the work and their budget.

Don't do it for free. That makes them devalue your work, and does a disservice to other poets who are trying to get paid. If they simply don't have a budget, then ask if you can put together a small grant application to the Arts Council on their behalf. The Arts Council exists to give artists money. A small grant can give you a few days' work and raise your profile.

Working in schools can be a good source of income. Put together an hour-long session that will teach basic poetry skills, and offer it to your local schools who may have a budget for it. If you can make it cross-curricular so that they are writing about physics, the local environment or history then so much the better. In the same way, tap into local events such as conferences, food festivals or open days at local attractions. Offer to be a poet in residence, sitting in on sessions and writing a short poem to sum up the proceedings. You will most likely need a DBS (Disclosure and Barring Service) check to work in schools, and some schools and community organisations or charities may also ask you for public liability insurance before employing you or allowing you to work in or hire their spaces for workshops. Fear not though, as these can easily be arranged by becoming a member of NAWE (the National Association of Writers in Education) who offer very affordable provision of such necessities to working writers. Their e-newsletter, The Writer's Compass, is also a valuable source of news, jobs and opportunities.

Getting paid to write a poem you actually *want* to write is rare. Commercial organisations, if they want a poem at all, will want one which delivers their own message. These commissions can be challenging, lucrative and – if you handle them well – creatively rewarding. Find an angle on the subject which is interesting in your own terms, so that you can write with some integrity even if the subject is cheap furniture. Make sure that the clients understand you are a creative writer, not a copywriter. Be ready to revise your first poem, but specify that they will only be entitled to one or two revisions; otherwise you may spend days or weeks reworking a poem to their satisfaction, and make no money at all.

Given that we struggle to find paid work, it's remarkable how bad we are at actually getting paid when we find it. The first step to getting paid is to understand this: you are not *lucky* to be working as a poet. Like a professional footballer or signwriter, you are making a living out of your skill. You are entitled to be paid. You will encounter many people who want a professional event such as a day's poetry workshop at a local stately home, and are surprised to hear that you expect to be paid. They assume that writing, particularly poetry, is a hobby. For many people it is; but at the stage where you are offering to run a workshop, deliver a one-woman show or work with children in a school, they should expect to pay you.

Ignore those who sniff at the jobbing poet. If we subscribe to the idea that poets should be 'above' taking money for their art, then we perpetuate the idea that good writing should never be paid for. That leaves poetry in the safe and steady hands of those who do not need to be paid for it. If musicians can write advertising jingles and Brian Eno can write the Microsoft 'welcome' sound, then writers' skills too should be valued in the terms which society understands best. If it was good enough for Auden, then it's good enough for the likes of you and me. This is a bigger issue than your pay packet or mine. Poets of all classes and backgrounds need to be represented in our schools, our institutions and our publications. There is no shame in doing something well for a commercial client, and getting paid for it.

Here are some of the responses you will hear when you ask for a fee, and the replies you might give. Don't for goodness' sake actually give these replies, which are the blunt ones that go through my head when yet another independently wealthy person or well-meaning volunteer asks me to work for free. Tone them down a bit.

We are a small charity – I am not.

It will be good for exposure – It may well be, but you're asking me to do a job.

The man who did it last year didn't ask to be paid – Can it be that you are now booking someone else because he wasn't very good?

We don't have a large budget – Look at your strategy. You can charge more for tickets, or get funding from elsewhere. I'll be happy to talk to you again when you have funding in place, or even help you to write a funding application.

We aren't paid ourselves – Good for you; I'm not in a position to work for free.

We are paid ourselves, but we don't pay writers – Goodbye.

CHAPTER THIRTY
When 'Poet' Will Never Be Your Only Title
by Abi Palmer

When I read about the literary routines of other writers, I feel cowed. There are poets who manage to sit at clean desks every day; who write in coffee shops; who work on vintage typewriters and embrace the clarity of a blank page. There are poets who talk about the physical relationship between movement and writing; who use the rhythm of walking or cycling; who clear their heads with the early morning air, building a poem slowly through clarity and freedom of movement.

I will never be one of these poets. I admire this discipline, but it has taken a long time to understand that poetry doesn't have to look like any of this. Of all literary forms, poetry is possibly the most flexible. It can be smaller than a haiku, or vaster and more unwieldy than anything by Dante. But if this is true, it follows there should be a way for it to expand and contract to your own experience. Not only the pains of a broken heart, or the patter of a new family, but to disability, anxiety and mental illness; to the limited resources of the overworked, the underpaid; to those of us who have caring responsibilities, dominant relationships or life experiences that make it hard to put our literary 'selves' first. There are those of us who are struggling with a sense of identity altogether, the task of establishing exactly what their 'self' may be. Some of us are unable to hold a book, to sit at a desk, or to even leave a house. We are all allowed to be poets too.

I have written before about the rising movement of D/deaf and/or disabled poets, for whom acknowledging the intrusion of daily lived experience may be used to produce interdisciplinary literary innovations[3]. But demanding that the form of your literary practice flexes to the demands of your lived experience is a method that I would invite any writer who is struggling to balance multiple roles to consider. Working *with,* rather than *in spite of* the intrusions placed upon your literary practice feels like a far more reasonable way for your work to develop.

In my own case, my project 'Alchemy'[4] came about, partly through frustration with not having the strength to hold a pen for long enough to craft new poems, but maintaining a desire to keep on exploring how far I could play with the limits of language and metaphor. I pushed my work in a different direction, taking four previously-completed poems, and inviting audiences to combine each one with an additional physical element (e.g. the smell of smoke, the touch of earth rubbed slowly into palms, a menthol sweet and a deep inhalation...). By combining four variable physical interactions, I was able to produce sixteen new performances from four old bits of writing. Since I was especially short on energy, in time I outsourced the physical exertion of performing even further, posting out the experiment as an 'interactive boxset' and inviting audiences to collaborate, feedback, and explore combinations in their own time. It is worth acknowledging that I had the support of a care assistant to complete these tasks.

'Upcycling' in this manner has yet to take the literary community by storm, but if you are short in capacity to craft an entire new poem, it is certainly worth considering. How does old work change when placed over a backdrop, into a collage, next to a movement, or alongside the soundtrack of a soap opera? Does a conflicting physical sensation push the poem in

---

3.　　　　Alland, Barokka and Sluman (Ed.s) *Stairs and Whispers: D/deaf and Disabled Poets Write Back* (Nine Arches Press, 2017)

4.　　　　For more information on the Alchemy project, please see: https://meetmytongue.tumblr.com/post/130683341248/the-alchemists-chest In boxset form: https://meetmytongue.tumblr.com/post/138741297983/alchemy-the-boxset (currently unavailable for sale but illustrates multiple forms)

a more interesting direction, or provide a new perspective? Is the effect banal, profound, or indifferent?

If you are feeling brave enough, you can invite friends and peers to transform your work for you, either in person, or through inviting social media to take your poem and place it into new contexts. Give your poem space to become irreverent, unwieldy, even obscene. How does it transform your experience? Voila: new work, as well as an expanded community.

There are other ways, too, to reuse and recycle. Raymond Queneau's *Exercises in Style* takes one fictional story and transforms it 99 times into different forms: a portrait, a letter, a series of elaborate metaphors...[5] This is one of my favourite forms of constraint, especially for the poet who is highly limited by their other 'selves'. If you work a 60-hour week but make the same journey every day, is there a way you might manage to repeatedly describe one element of it? A street? The smell of a bus? The jostling of bodies on trains? If you are indoors a lot, how many ways can you describe the same piece of wall or ceiling? What happens if you restrict word count or writing time? Finding fleeting, formal or informal ways to retell the same experience, or capture how a similar experience varies from day to day is a continuous exploration of the vast potential of language, one moment at a time. You may never move beyond a line a day (or less still), but be prepared for a poem which starts growing itself.

An all-too common refrain in for much of adult life is 'I haven't got time for this.' But the more compromised your body, your mind, or your wallet may be, the more I would argue for practices that openly embrace relinquishing control (if even for the briefest of moments). Techniques such as cut-ups, erasures, and re-translations are all useful ways to relieve the pressure of starting with a blank page that can be finished quickly, yet provide infinite and unexpected possibilities.

5.　　　Raymond Queneau – *Exercises in Style* (New Directions, 2013)

Exquisite corpses are a useful way to incorporate poetry writing into caring responsibilities or motherhood: how does a poem change when your four year-old has added the next line? If you have half a drafted poem that never went where you wanted it to, what happens when you spin it off in a totally different direction? Can you switch forms, include a picture, a line of instructions, or a ripped page? Can you search for meaning where you meant none?

This brings me to the primary conclusion of this briefest of prompt sheets for the compromised writer: play. Give yourself permission, more permission than you believe you deserve, to explore without consequence. To me, the mark of a real poet is not necessarily measurable by volume of work, or number of accolades, but on the relationship the writer holds to their own practice. No matter what your limitations, it is vital to allow permission, occasionally, for your work to be inconsequential: to make a mess and then see what comes out of it. Writing needn't be tamed into a grey-suited 9-5, or get up every morning before the sun rises. Some poetry might be more comfortable tucked up in bed, in yesterday's tracksuit, or perhaps, sporadically, cartwheeling across the page. Allow space for your practice to flex to the world you inhabit. Just don't be afraid when your work starts flexing back.

Abi Palmer is an interactive writer and artist. Her multisensory poetry installation 'Alchemy' was awarded Best Wildcard at the Saboteur Literary Awards 2016. She is currently working on a 10 month project 'Sanatorium,' exploring the relationship between language, pain, and the body, funded by Arts Council England. Her essay 'No Body to Write With: Intrusion as a Manifesto for D/deaf and Disabled Writers' was published in *Stairs and Whispers: D/deaf and Disabled Poets Write Back* (Nine Arches Press, 2017). www.abipalmer.com @abipalmer_bot

CHAPTER THIRTY-ONE
How to Go Live:
Performing and Reading Your Poems

When I think of the best live poetry I have experienced, I think of the times where a poet's performance has left an indelible mark on me. Where the reading has brought the poem to life in startling and electrifying ways; those moments when I first heard a life-changing poem, or when the audience was hushed by the subtle magic of a striking, careful or astounding voice as it delivers a poem and lets it glitter, real and alive and aloud in the air between us. There are several poets I've gone on to publish whose initial readings truly captivated me, and many more I'd queue up to hear read, time after time, because I know something incredible will happen in their performing and releasing of their poems.

For me, the hearing of a poem read or performed well will change the poem forever for me, inextricably linking the printed and heard words. I will 'hear' the poem on the page in my 'mind's ear' when I read the poems again to myself, illuminated with the poet's own way of putting things now resounding as I'm reading.

I've heard poets at local events or small open mics reading for the very first time whose poems have blown everything else off the stage. I've also heard top-flight poets at large events who have flattened a favourite poem to a drone, or left me feeling rather disappointed or nonplussed.

Let me bring this back to you, reader; you may have read or performed your poems plenty of times before, or never at all. You may feel quite comfortable and confident, or utterly terrified or bit shaky at the prospect.

You will notice in what follows that I refer to 'reading or performing' your poems. I make this open form of distinction here, as I know some of you will feel you firmly belong in the camp of one or other of these definitions – and may perhaps clearly identify yourself as a 'performance' poet or a 'page' poet with some certainty. Some of you may feel that your poems exist simultaneously between the read and the performed depending on 'which' poems and 'which' context, and others amongst you will perhaps feel that there's a bit more of an interchangeability here, a certain degree of slippage between what you feel you're doing when you get in front of an audience and give voice to your words. This is all to say that however you want to define what you do is fine, and I use the terms here together so as not to exclude anyone. After all, it really doesn't matter so long as you feel at home as a 'reader' or a 'performer' or 'spoken word artist' or even perhaps simply a 'live poet'. Here's to live poetry, and all the good things that happen when we give some volume to our words and the oxygen of a live space to air them in when we let them be heard.

With that in mind, let's step up to the microphone with seventeen handy tips on getting the best from your open mic and poetry performance:

1. Don't be afraid of the microphone
Speak directly into the microphone, and avoid speaking into the side or over the top, as it will not pick up your voice as clearly. Ideally, your mouth should be level and about 3-4 inches from the top 'crown' of the microphone. A microphone has a sensitive diaphragm inside, and for optimal pick-up you need to read closely and directly into the centre of it.

2. Do take the time to adjust the microphone and stand
Make sure the stand is adjusted to your height. Stand in front of the mic centrally, try not to twist your body towards or away from it as this will be uncomfortable. Take your time, and ask the compere or host if you need a hand to make the adjustments.

3. Don't point the mic downwards

Time after time, I see readers adjust a mic either towards their book or feet, or step backwards and away from the mic. It won't pick up your voice clearly like this; get close and direct.

4. Don't say 'I don't need to use the mic'

Or 'I don't like microphones, so I won't bother' – please always use a mic if it's provided. You may not be able to project your voice as well as you think, and bear in mind that some people in your audience may be D/deaf or have impaired hearing and be reliant on your use of the mic for them to hear you clearly, especially where there is background noise. Not using a mic can also cause you to over-strain your voice, or to shout the poems rather than read them more naturally.

5. Don't outstay your welcome

If you don't know how many poems you are expected to read at an open mic, ask the host. It's rare for any open mic slot to welcome more than two poems on the open mic. Also, don't say 'I know it's only two poems, but I'm going to read five short ones.' Two poems means two poems.

If you are invited to an event or festival to give a reading, ask in advance how long you're expected to be reading for. Prepare your poems and practise reading them through whilst timing if it's useful to know how long they will take to read or perform live. Take a watch or a phone with you to keep an eye on the time if you need to. Read your poems at your normal pace, without rushing to cram in more than you can comfortably read in the allotted time.

Some years ago, I sat through a one-hour festival reading of three poets, where the first poet read for half an hour without being stopped. The two poets who followed ended up with less than ten minutes each to read, after introductions. It felt rude and disrespectful to those other readers, and to the audience (who were fidgeting in their seats as the reading overran) and it didn't leave a good impression of that poet.

Remember: no one comes away from a poetry event and is glad that it went on for far too long. If in doubt, err on the side of a shorter performance, and fewer poems – it is after all, better to leave your audience wanting more.

6. Read the poems in your own voice

Don't use a pretend accent, silly voice or imitations. Don't put on a 'poetry voice' to read your poems. Adopting this voice is a bit like putting on a special 'telephone voice' to perform or read and it will feel (and sound) unnatural.

Be proud of your voice, with all of its inflections, accents, dialects, breathing patterns and idiosyncrasies, and put this at the heart of reading or performing your poems. Use the whole of your own voice; inhabit it and trust in it to be strong enough to convey the poem. Read like you mean it because, in all honesty, if these are good poems and you believe in them and want others to believe in them, you *should* mean it.

7. Be organised

Have your poems to hand and ready to read, and don't take up time changing your mind and flicking through sheaves of paper or notebooks. Print your poems out if reading them from paper, or put them into a folder or booklet to keep them together. If you have a book or pamphlet, read from it – it's good for audiences to see they can buy the publication from you afterwards; it's also useful for your publisher, and shows off your book if photographs are taken for social media or promotional purposes.

8. Don't read something you have only just written ten minutes before the event started

And don't apologise and tell the audience you're about to read something you wrote ten minutes before the event started.

9. Don't apologise about reading your poems, full stop

Fledgling poets are often known to be self-deprecating, but never begin a reading by apologising for being there, or saying your poem 'isn't very good' or putting yourself or your poems down. It is often done out of nervousness, or to break the ice, but instead it acts as a form of self-sabotage. You have as much right as anyone else there to be on the mic, reading your poems, and nothing to apologise for.

10. Don't proffer unsolicited advice

Avoid critique of fellow readers, and be cautious of those offering it unless they are trusted listeners who know your work well and are offering fair and thoughtful feedback. It can be damaging to take on board bad advice, or to start tailoring your work towards the one critical voice at your open mic that, for instance, prefers comedic verse and tells you that you should *go and write some funny ones, crowd-pleasers that the audience can laugh along with*. I was given this very advice at the first live event I ever read a poem at when I was nineteen. I'm glad I ignored it.

11. Do be supportive

Cheer others on, applaud, and do tell them when a poem has genuinely bowled you over. It matters a lot to all of us coming up through all the various areas of poetry performance to know this.

12. Don't turn up, insist on an early slot, read your poem and then leave

You'd be amazed how many people do this at open mics – I've even seen readers walk away from the mic, pack their things away noisily and clamber over the rest of audience to leave mid-reading. If an audience is doing you the courtesy of listening to your poems, you should be prepared to stay and listen to the other readers also.

13. Don't give an over-long explanation or introduction before reading the poem

Though there are some accomplished poets who give entertaining, funny or informative preliminaries which segue skilfully between poems, or tell a story relevant to a poem, it is rarely something you will need to do at your local open mic. If it is necessary (i.e. to give the meaning of a word in a poem, or origin of a phrase or epigram on the page) do explain but don't go into the sort of excessive detail and explanation that will render the reading of the poem unnecessary by the time you're done. If it's not in the poem already, and the poem won't make sense without it, this raises a question as to whether it needs to be, and if your poem is working as well as it should do? Are you trusting in your audience to be smart enough to 'get' the poem, or not?

14. Do look up and look out at the audience as you read

You don't have to make direct eye contact with audience members, and if there are bright stage lights it may not be possible to anyway – but looking out towards your listeners brings your audience *in* and can help you to project your poem outwards.

Nervous about reading to an audience? That's perfectly natural, so why not try this tip: look out not into the eyes of individuals, but focus just above the eyebrows to the foreheads or hairlines of your audience. A general focus as just above eye level will create a more relaxing sense of a general crowd of people in front of you, making you feel less anxious about looking at any one person, but will still give the impression you are looking out into the audience and reading your poems to them. Or, if that doesn't work for you, pick a non-human focal point in the middle distance of the room (a picture in the wall or a part of the backdrop), again just above the audience's heads, and read out to this point.

15. Do use a music stand or a lectern if you find it useful

Perhaps bring a small folding stand with you if you find it allows you to read more easily or make eye contact with audiences. Alternatively, move lecterns or stands out of the way if you feel they get in between you and the audience. Do what works best for you, in other words.

16. Do take your time and read clearly

Don't feel pressured to rush through your poems, and let your audience have time to hear them clearly. This is another good reason not to cram too many poems in.

17. Be choosy

It's important to find events that are welcoming and positive places to share your poetry. Maybe attend first and check out a poetry event before reading there in order to make sure it's the right kind of event for you, or ask for recommendations. Some events may be really friendly, but you may feel your type of poems wouldn't work there – in which case, you could just go along and enjoy being an audience member, cheering on the talent of others. However, heckling, harassment, bullying or any other disrespectful, negative or discriminatory behaviour should not be tolerated at any good, well-run poetry event or open mic. Don't attend an event if you don't feel confident that the atmosphere of an event is as safe, friendly or supportive as it should be, and don't feel you have to stay and read a poem if you've signed up for a slot on the open mic but something doesn't feel right to you. Your instincts matter – and there are plenty more good, welcoming events out there where you and your poems will be better appreciated and respected.

Finally, a quick footnote, after all this talk of reading and performing your poems. If you don't perform or read your poetry live, it is entirely your rightful decision to make, and no one should ever feel they *have* to read their poems or perform them live to be a poet. It is perfectly valid to feel that you are not the best performer of your work, to recognise that you do not feel happy or comfortable performing your poems live, or to know that you are not able to, and ask others to respect that.

There are other options open to you; these may include recording, filming or podcasting your poems or recording other people reading them for you, or to blog, share and publish them online or in journals, pamphlets and books, and for this to be the mode in which your work mainly seeks and finds an audience. Reading and performing your poetry live is only one way of getting your poems out there.

CHAPTER THIRTY-TWO
On Social Media

By the time I've finished writing this paragraph, some new social media platform will have popped up. Things change quickly but Facebook, Twitter and the rest are vital tools to share news of your work, to gather news about events and competitions, and to generate interest in events you've organised. Beyond self-interest, they allow us to build a real poetry community. We've said that 'being a poet' is about more than writing poetry. Social media give us a real opportunity to meet other poets. We find online courses or real-world writing groups; we learn about other kinds of writing and discover new voices. Some of those 'friends' become actual friends.

We can only give a few tips here, for the less confident swimmer in digital waters. The first is: *be generous*. Social media is not advertising, it's a conversation – hence the 'social'. If every post concerns your own work, your own readings, the nice thing somebody said about your pamphlet, a picture of you at a reading last night, then your conversation becomes dull. People stop reading your posts. As a rule of thumb, write four out of five posts about somebody else. If you see news of a poetry competition, a good article or a local event in your news feed, a crowd-funding campaign that benefits poetry, then press 'share' and spread the word to your readership. In addition to these posts, you will of course shout about your own up-and-coming readings, your good fortune in competitions, or your queries about what Indian poetry to read.

Build a useful network by following people who interest you, and looking at who they themselves follow. Don't feel guilty about muting or unfollowing those people who bore or irritate you. You should be reading a news feed full of relevant and interesting information. It should feel like walking down the high street of a lively village, not dodging bullets in Sniper Alley.

If you're nervous about social media, remember that you won't break the computer by having a go. Each platform has its own idiosyncrasies. Take the trouble to spend half an hour in the 'settings' or 'how to' section, to learn the possibilities of each application. If you are bombarded with notifications from Twitter, for example – *turn them off*. On Facebook you can turn off notifications for every post, so you won't be troubled by people adding their personal thoughts on the Forward Prize. Learn how to limit your posts on Facebook to a specific audience, so that pictures of your sexy Hallowe'en costume are not shared with the director of the Poetry Society.

There are some important rules for etiquette. Twitter allows you to contact your writing heroes directly, but don't ever hijack the feed of a writer or publisher you admire with a post like this: 'Love your work Nikesh. Check out my video on YouTube'. It's discourteous and lazy. Don't message a poet to ask if they will read your work without payment. A friend of mine tweeted this week to announce that she had completed her PhD. 'Fantastic news,' replied a stranger, 'will you read my novel please?' From a friend, that would be a big ask. From a stranger it's simply rude. By all means ask for guidance on what to do with an unpublished manuscript, but be aware that your message may be one of many.

Please do not share a picture of someone else's poem from a book, or worse still copy it out and post it. You mean it as a compliment, but it is a breach of copyright and a small theft. Such an image can easily be lifted and circulated without attribution. Thousands of people may enjoy, copy or plagiarise the work without the poet getting any benefit or exposure. I've had people plagiarise my work from an unattributed image, and had criticism for writing bad poetry when someone actually tweeted half of the poem or got the line breaks wrong. Instead, quote a couple of lines and share a link to the poet's web page. In that way you compliment them and send other fans directly to their work, rather than circulating it with no benefit to the writer.

By the same token, if you put up your own poem on the internet (even on your own blog or Facebook page) then you are publishing it worldwide. It immediately becomes ineligible for competitions or submitting to journals. Some people get around this by removing the offending material from their page as soon as it is accepted for publication. However, it may have been shared widely already. This matters, because a journal which has accepted your poem in good faith wants to be the first to publish it. The editors are building their own reputation for good taste and fresh work. Competitions, likewise, insist on work being unpublished so if you're planning to submit it to the National Poetry Competition, do not share it with the world. Somewhere in that world are the judges of the National Poetry Competition, and if they see your poem then it is no longer anonymous.

Use the Facebook 'Event' feature to make your poetry reading or pamphlet launch an actual event. This makes it much easier for others to spread the word, gives them a map of the venue and allows you to see how many people are coming. On Twitter, you can mute people without unfollowing them. On Instagram you can share photos of your lively audiences or lovely venues without further embellishment.

Whatever media you use, take time to learn their strengths and enjoy them.

CHAPTER THIRTY-THREE
The Final Word

Dear poets, we release you now into the wild, to the pages, stages, and digital spaces where poetry is flourishing in the twenty-first century. We hope that you thrive and prosper – whether by publishing, performing or simply by being a poet and participating in this art form as a reader and writer.

We hope that our advice and the insight of our seven special-guest essayists will pay you dividends in the long term. As always, we hope that our ideas help and guide you but do not bind you; as Jo's big ruthless list advises, take a healthy pinch of salt with these words. Listen to as many voices of poetry expertise as you can, don't just take our word for it.

If we leave you with one thing, it is to say that you must continue to grant yourself permission. Don't let self-doubt waylay you, but rather put it to work productively in helping you to strive towards writing better every time. Don't be afraid either to make rules for yourself and your poetry, or to bend or break those same rules when you need to push your creative capabilities further. Once you've built the room of a poem, you can always push the walls out and get a better view of what's beyond, and what is fully possible. You have permission. You can do this.

More than anything, persist. Keep going, keep on reading, writing, and redrafting. Don't neglect the kind of active and attentive listening, looking and pondering about things that is also valuable to the work of a poet. The only way to be a poet is to get on with it.

So, what are you waiting for?

Jo Bell's Big Ruthless List
for Poetry Writing*

1. Get rid of cliché. All of it.

2. Forbidden words*: shard, gossamer, soul, upon (nobody says 'upon'), eternity, iridescent, love.

3. Get rid of abstracts – love, passion, joy, ecstasy. A writer's work is to make me feel it, not to tell me that you felt it. *Show* it with the five senses instead. 'Loneliness' can be shown by a single cup on the draining board where there used to be two.

4. Never, ever invert word order to sound poetic. You are not Yoda.

5. Take out any word that is there solely to fit a rhyme scheme or meter. *We can tell.*

6. Is every word earning its keep? If not, bin it – including *and* and *the* – without making sentences stilted.

7. Could your lines be broken differently? If so, you haven't finished yet.

8. Is there *any* rhythm, rhyme, pattern or structure? If not, you are writing prose.

9. Look at the beginning and end of the piece. Can you cut two lines at each end, and make no difference? Do it.

10. Are you assuming your reader is more stupid than you? Don't.

11. Are you assuming your reader is more intelligent than you? Don't.

12. Is your poem boring? Consider approach, pace, point of view and imagery.

13. Expose yourself – a poem should cost you something to write. You can't hold on to your dignity and be believed all the time.

14. What's the *point* of your poem – is it purely a personal snapshot?

15. Be true, rather than accurate. Change names, locations etc., if necessary.

16. Form. If you are using a form, why?

17. Form. If you are not using a form, why not?

18. Could this poem have been written by anyone, or is it definitely yours?

19. If you think you can get away with it, you can't.

20. 'Good enough' isn't good enough. Keep editing until it is as good as it can be, has something to say and says it your way.

*To be consumed with a pinch of salt

Jane Commane's Top Ten Tips for Good Poetry Practice

1. Read widely.

2. Write adventurously.

3. Edit and redraft thoroughly.

4. Grant yourself permission. Don't be afraid of making and breaking rules.

5. Think and ruminate on poems, both the ones you write and the ones you read. Like bread and beer, they'll always be better for the fermentation process.

6. Be a generous and genuine encourager of others: share opportunities and good news, open doors, make space. Be glad for others when they succeed.

7. Participate. Make a positive contribution to the ecosystem and community of writing in your own way.

8. Tune in to your own voice: believe in its possibilities, and know that it is strong enough to carry your poem.

9. Be patient and take your time. It will always take longer than you think, but it will be worth the wait.

10. Don't get too comfortable. Push at your creative limits and at your own ideas of what your writing is capable of. Keep working away at being a better poet.

Resources for Poets

This list is by no means exhaustive, but contains links to a number of organisations and online resources which we thought may be useful or have been referred to in these chapters.

Visit the *How to be a Poet* blog at: www.howtobeapoet.com

Online Resources
The Poetry Foundation: www.poetryfoundation.org
The Poetry Archive: www.poetryarchive.org
Poetry Magazines: www.poetrymagazines.org.uk
Lunar Poetry Podcasts: www.lunarpoetrypodcasts.com

Useful Poetry Organisations
The Poetry Society: www.poetrysociety.org.uk
The Poetry Book Society: www.poetrybooks.co.uk
Forward Arts Foundation: www.forwardartsfoundation.org
Apples and Snakes: www.applesandsnakes.org

Libraries, Archives and Resources
The National Poetry Library: www.poetrylibrary.org.uk
The Scottish Poetry Library: www.scottishpoetrylibrary.org.uk

Writer Development and Workshops
The Poetry School: www.poetryschool.com
The Poetry School's list of poets who offer mentoring, plus information on mentoring arrangements, tutorials and manuscript assessment services, can be found at: www.poetryschool.com/1-2-1/
The Literary Consultancy: www.literaryconsultancy.co.uk
Arvon Residential courses: www.arvon.org
Ty Newydd residential courses: www.tynewydd.wales
Moniack Mhor residential courses: www.moniackmhor.org.uk
The Poetry Business (regular writing workshops and more): www.poetrybusiness.co.uk

Professional Support for Poets

NAWE

The National Association of Writers in Education supports anyone who works in teaching and tutoring. Also, website includes the Writer's Compass resources (and membership will also include access to a very useful email newsletter full of news, competitions and opportunities for writers).
www.nawe.co.uk

The Writers' Guild

The Writers' Guild of Great Britain (WGGB) is a trade union representing professional writers in TV, film, theatre, radio, books, comedy, poetry, animation and video games. Their members also include emerging and aspiring writers.
www.writersguild.org.uk

The Society of Authors

A trade union for professional writers, illustrators and literary translators that also provides grants to fund works in progress and support authors in financial difficulty.
www.societyofauthors.org

Royal Literary Fund

The RLF is a UK charity providing grants and pensions to writers in financial difficulty. The RLF also runs a Fellowship scheme for writers in partnership with universities. Writers work one-to-one with students, using their expertise in language and communication to help them develop their essay writing.
www.rlf.org.uk

Funding Bodies

In the UK, Arts funding organisations do provide assistance and funding to support poetry activities, which may also include support for creative development and writing time for individuals. Please see the relevant funding body, and read the funding guidance on their websites. We also recommend going to the 'How to Apply for Funding' workshops which arts funding organisations do often provide through literature development agencies, or joining their mailing lists so you can stay up to date with news and opportunities.

Arts Council England: www.artscouncil.org.uk
Arts Council of Northern Ireland: www.artscouncil-ni.org
Creative Scotland: www.creativescotland.com
Arts Council of Wales: www.arts.wales

Regional and National Literary Development Agencies

Again, we strongly advise joining the mailing list for your local literature development agency, or following their social media accounts for news and opportunities.

Literature Works (south west): www.literatureworks.org.uk
Spread the Word (London): www.spreadtheword.org.uk
New Writing North: www.newwritingnorth.com
New Writing South (south east): www.newwritingsouth.com
Writer's Centre Norwich: www.writerscentrenorwich.org.uk
Writing West Midlands: www.writingwestmidlands.org
Writing East Midlands: www.writingeastmidlands.co.uk
Literature Wales: www.literaturewales.org

Other Useful Writing Guides and Handbooks

We recommend ordering these titles via your nearest friendly bookshop if you can, or with an independent online retailer such as Hive (www.hive.co.uk).

On Publishing

The Writer's and Artists' Yearbook (published annually by Bloomsbury).

Indie Presses 2016/17: The Mslexia Guide to Small and Independent Book Publishers and Literary Magazines in the UK and the Republic of Ireland (Mslexia, 2016, updated annually).

How ~~Not~~ to Publish Your Poetry – Helena Nelson (Happenstance Press, 2016).

101 Ways to Make Poems Sell: The Salt Guide to Getting and Staying Published (Salt Guides for Readers & Writers) by Chris Hamilton-Emery, (Salt Publishing, 2006).

On Writing

52: Write a Poem a Week. Start Now. Keep Going – Jo Bell (Nine Arches Press, 2015).

Adventures in Form A Compendium of New Poetic Forms – Tom Chivers (Penned in the Margins, 2012).

Cambridge Introduction to Creative Writing – David Morley (Cambridge Introductions to Literature, 2011).

Don't Ask Me What I Mean: Poets in Their Own Words – edited by Don Paterson and Clare Brown (Picador, 2012).

In Their Own Words: Contemporary Poets on their Poetry – Edited by Helen Ivory and George Szirtes (Salt Publishing, 2012).

On Poetry - Glyn Maxwell (Oberon Books, 2012 / 2017)

Poetry in the Making: A Handbook for Writing and Teaching – Ted Hughes (Faber & Faber 1967 / 2008).

Strong Words: Modern Poets on Modern Poetry – edited by W. N. Herbert and Matthew Hollis (Bloodaxe, 2000).

The Faith of a Writer: Life, Craft, Art – Joyce Carol Oates (Harper Collins 2009).

The Practice of Poetry: Writing Exercises From Poets Who Teach – edited by Robin Behn and Chase Twichell (William Morrow Paperbacks, 1992).

Writing Poems – Peter Sansom (Bloodaxe, 1993).

Writing Poetry – W. N. Herbert (Routledge, 2009).

Notes and Thanks

Some of these chapters appeared previously in earlier versions on our website at: www.howtobeapoet.com and on Jo Bell's blog at: www.belljarblog.wordpress.com.

We are most grateful to our wonderful contributors, Mona Arshi, Clive Birnie, Rishi Dastidar, Jonathan Davidson, Abi Palmer, Robert Peake and Joelle Taylor for their essays and for kindly granting us permission to feature and share their thoughts on a variety of poetry topics.

Many thanks are due to Kate Clanchy for kind permission to feature and reproduce her poem 'Patagonia'.

Thanks are also due to Arts Council England for funding and supporting the writing and development of this book, and to the Jerwood Compton Poetry Fellowship scheme, which has further supported Jane Commane in 2017-18.

Acknowledgements

David Bayles and Ted Orland: *Art & Fear: Observations on the Perils (and Rewards) of Artmaking* (Image Continuum Press, 2001).

Jo Bell: 'Mallaig' from *Kith* (Nine Arches Press, 2015).

David Bowie: quote from film interview 'Bowie's advice to Artists (1997)' as featured on YouTube: https://www.youtube.com/watch?v=h48hGHALFC4

Basil Bunting: *Briggflatts* (new edition) (Bloodaxe Books, 2009).

Kate Clanchy: 'Patagonia' from *Slattern* (Picador; 2001), reproduced with the kind permission of the poet.

Roy Peter Clark: *Writing Tools: 50 Essential Strategies for Every Writer* (Little, Brown and Company, 2008).

Ernest Hemingway: *With Hemingway: A Year in Key West and Cuba by Arnold Samuelson,* (Random House, 1984).

Mark Forsyth: *The Elements of Eloquence: How To Turn the Perfect English Phrase* (Icon Books Ltd, 2016).

Eugen Herrigel: *Zen in the Art of Archery* (Penguin, 1988).

Richard Hugo: *The Triggering Town* (W. W. Norton & Co, 2010).

Lewis Hyde: *The Gift: How the Creative Spirit Transforms the World* (Canongate Books, 2006).

Glyn Maxwell: *On Poetry* (Oberon Books, 2012 / 2017).

George Orwell: 'Politics and the English Language' from *Essays* (Penguin Modern Classics, 2 Jan 2014).

Sylvia Plath: *The Unabridged Journals of Sylvia Plath* (Anchor Books; 2000).

Shel Silverstein: *The Giving Tree* (HarperCollins, 2003).

Sol Stein: *Stein On Writing* (St. Martin's Griffin, 2000).

Wislawa Szymborska: as quoted from the Poetry Foundation website: https://www.poetryfoundation.org/articles/68657/how-to-and-how-not-to-write-poetry-56d2484397277